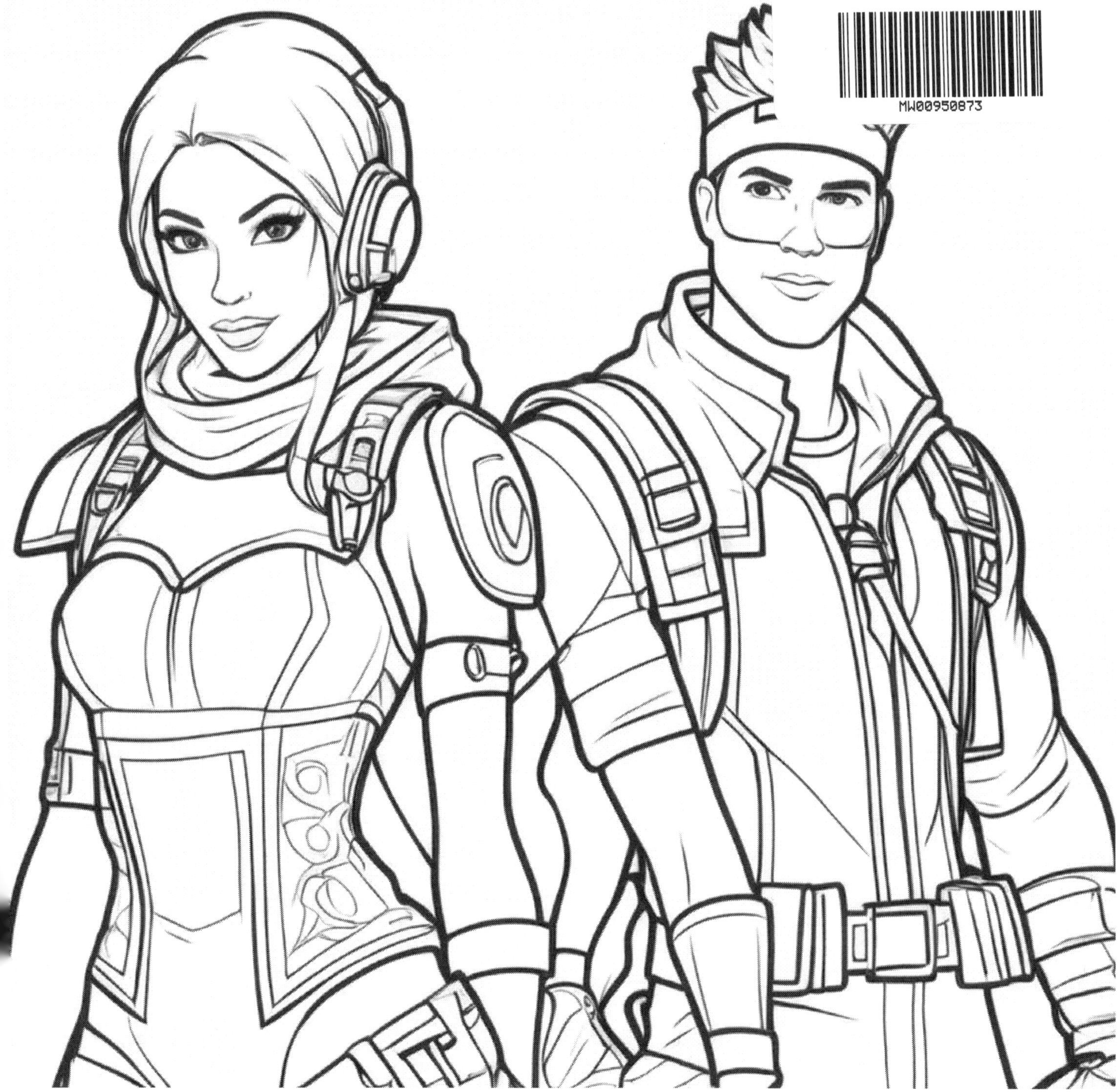

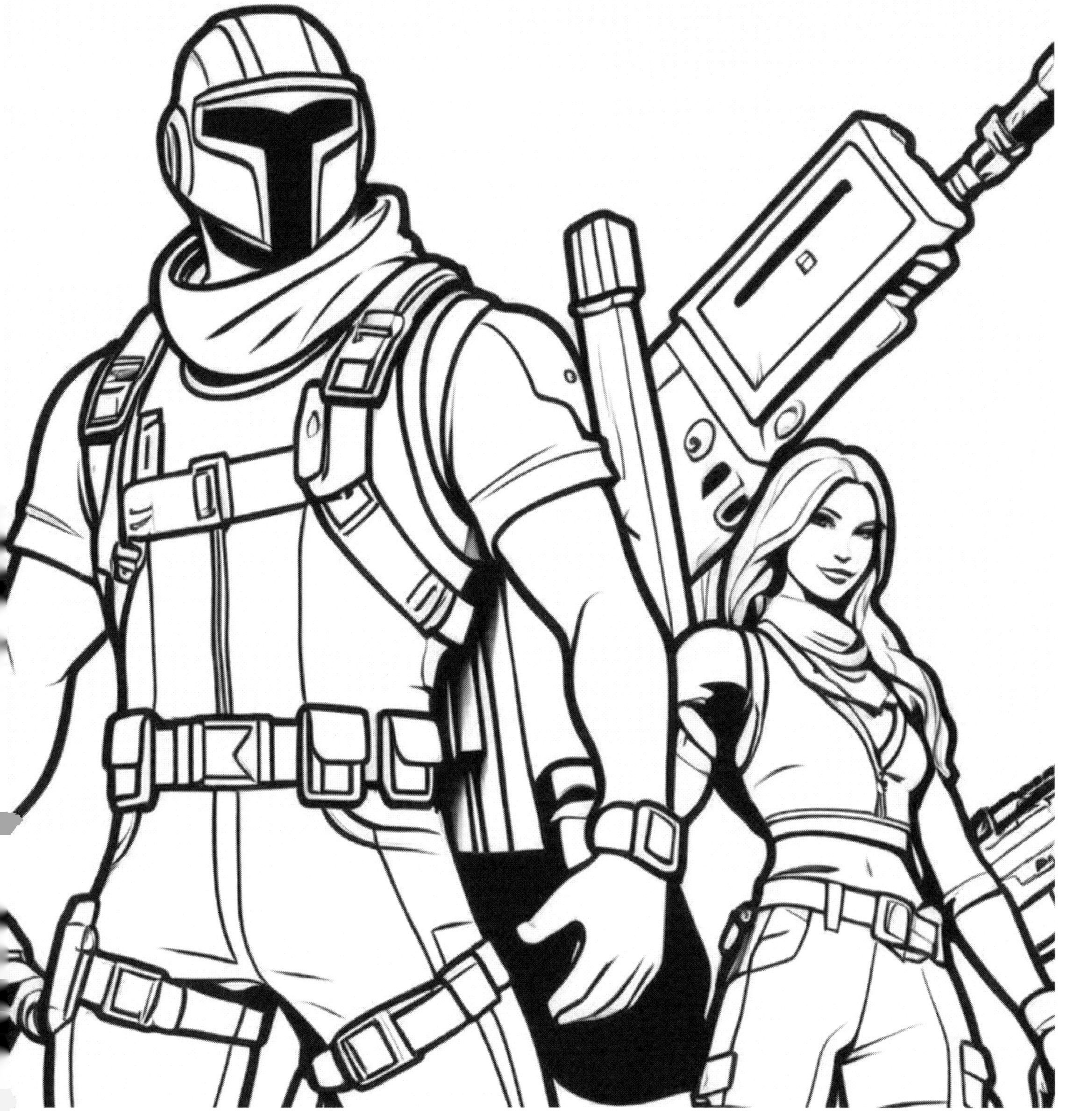

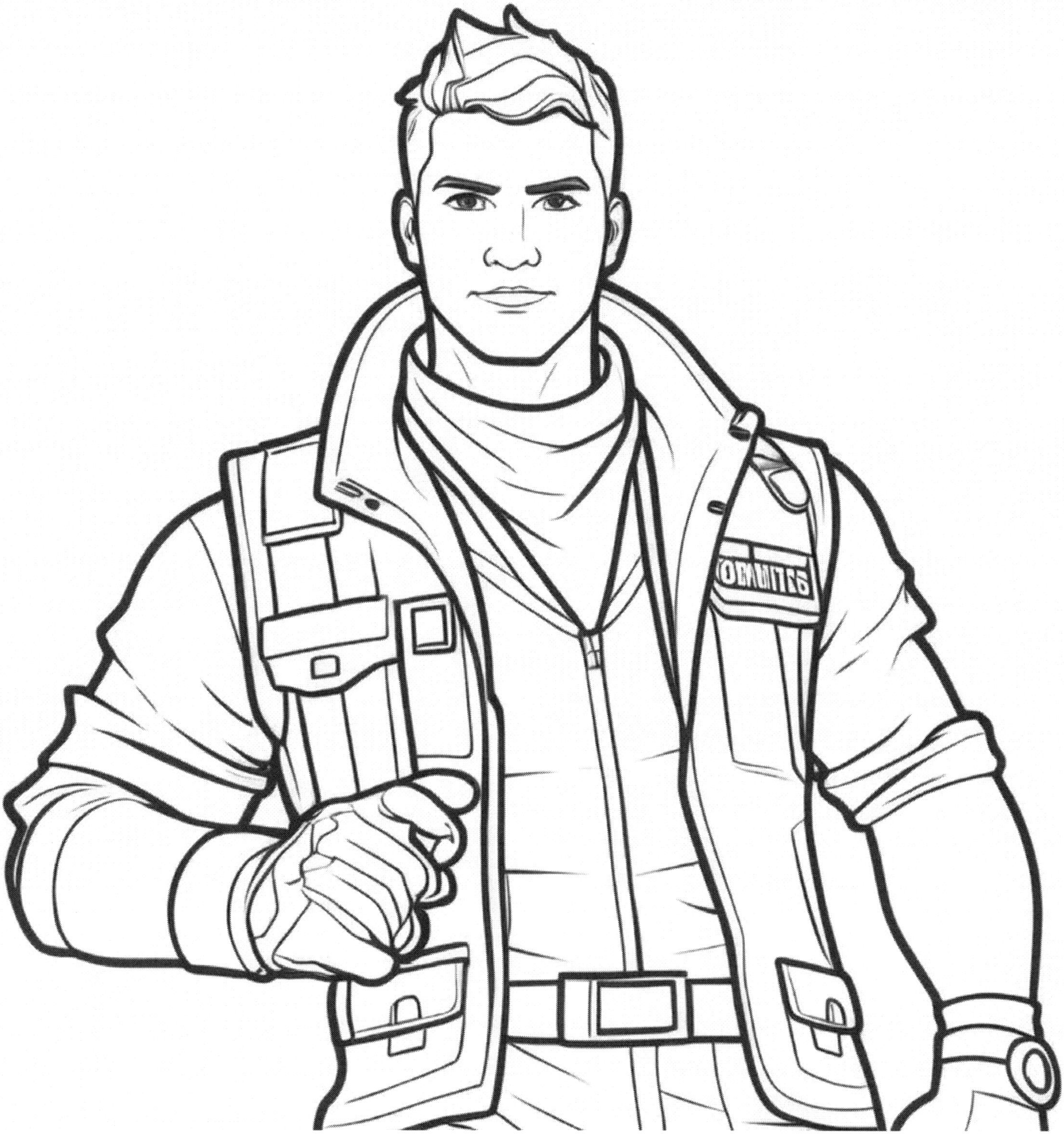

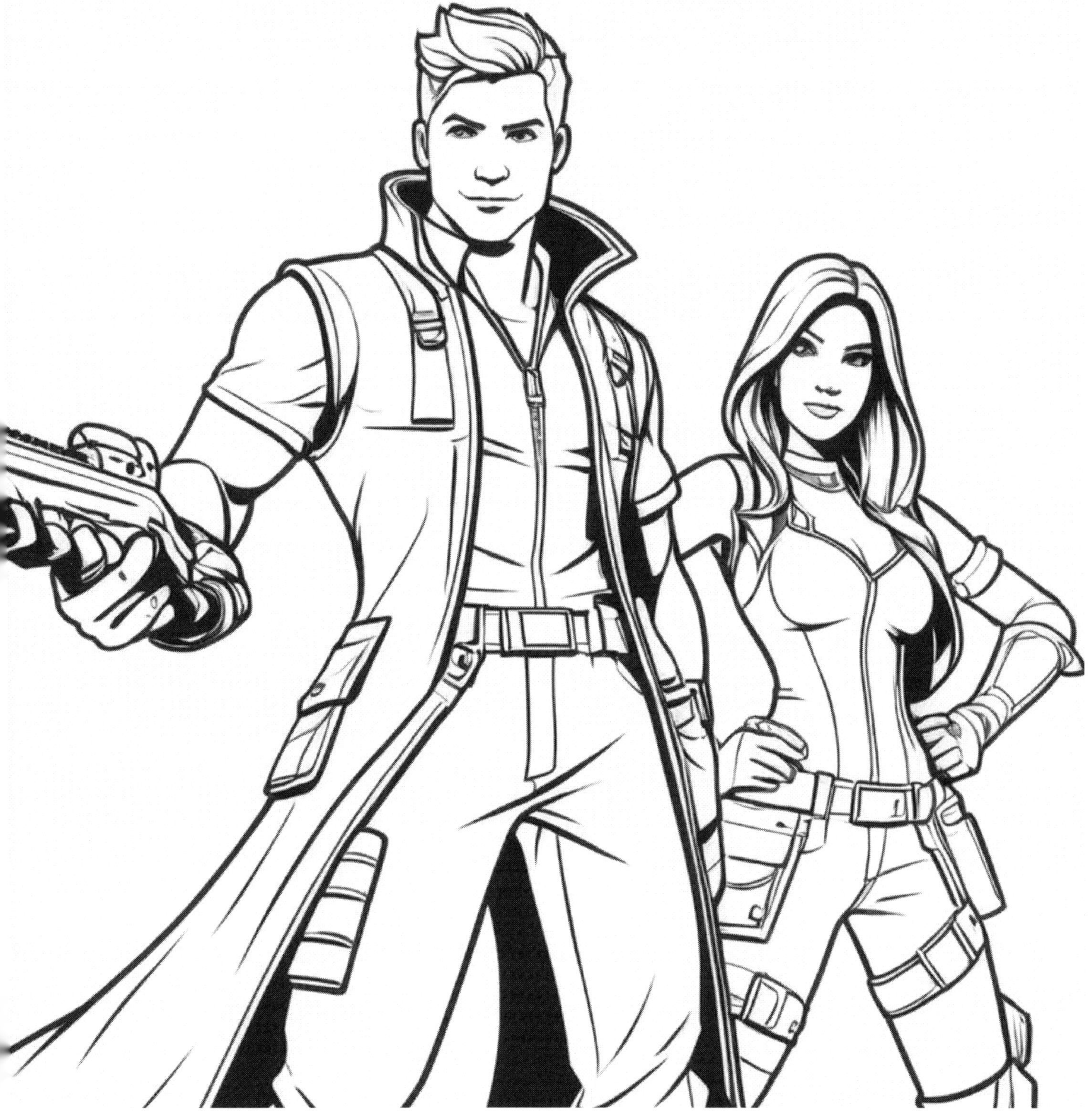

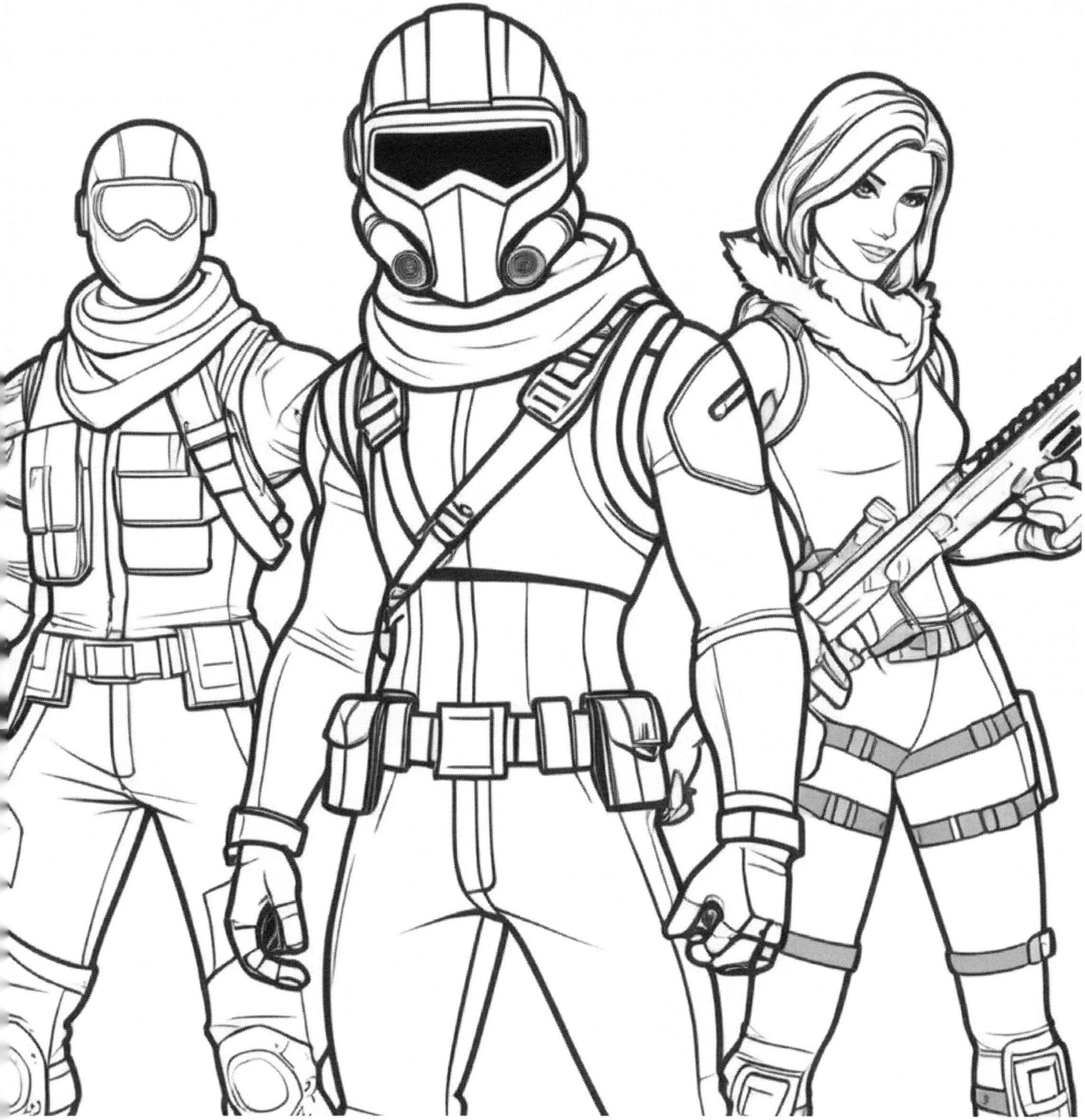

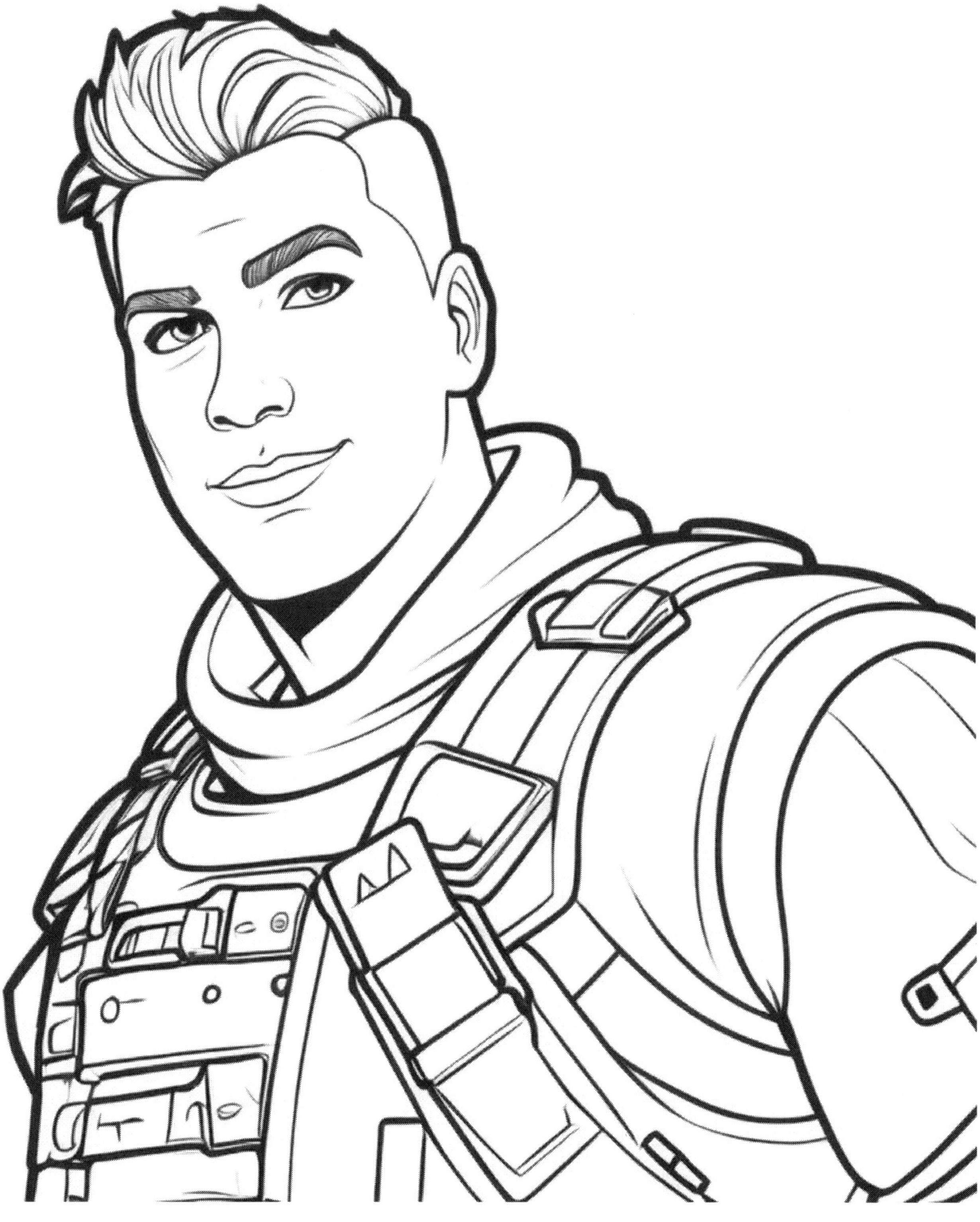

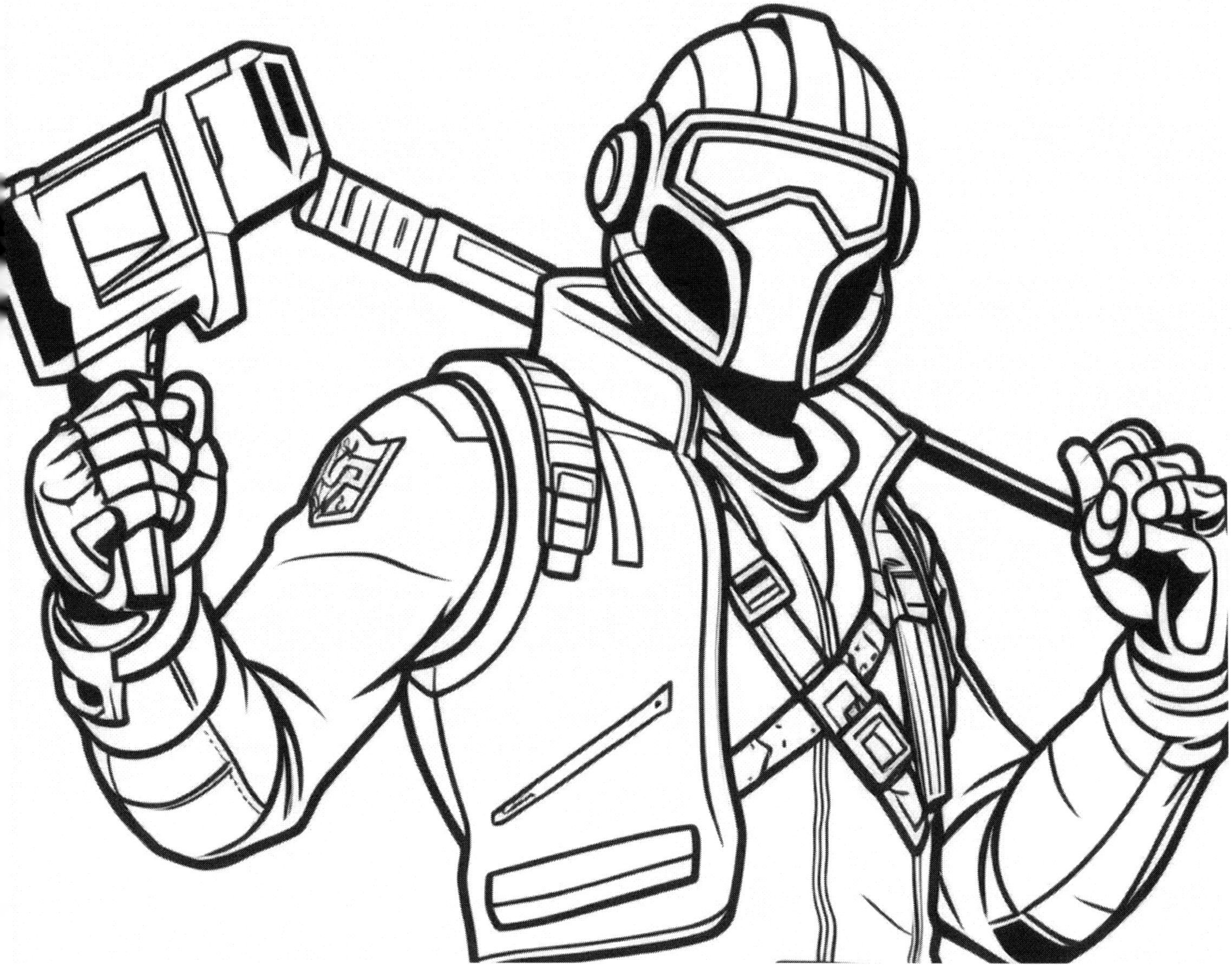

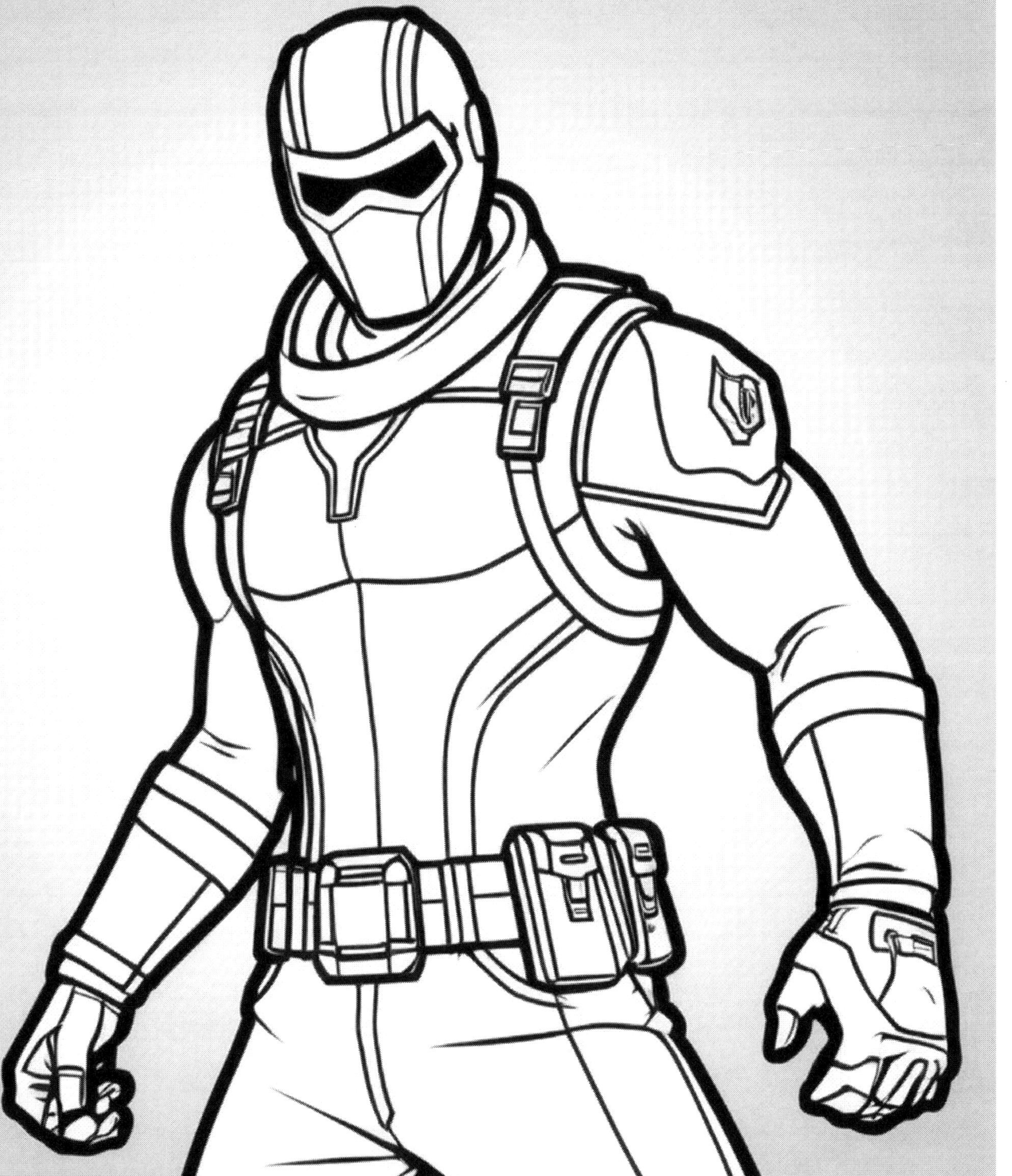

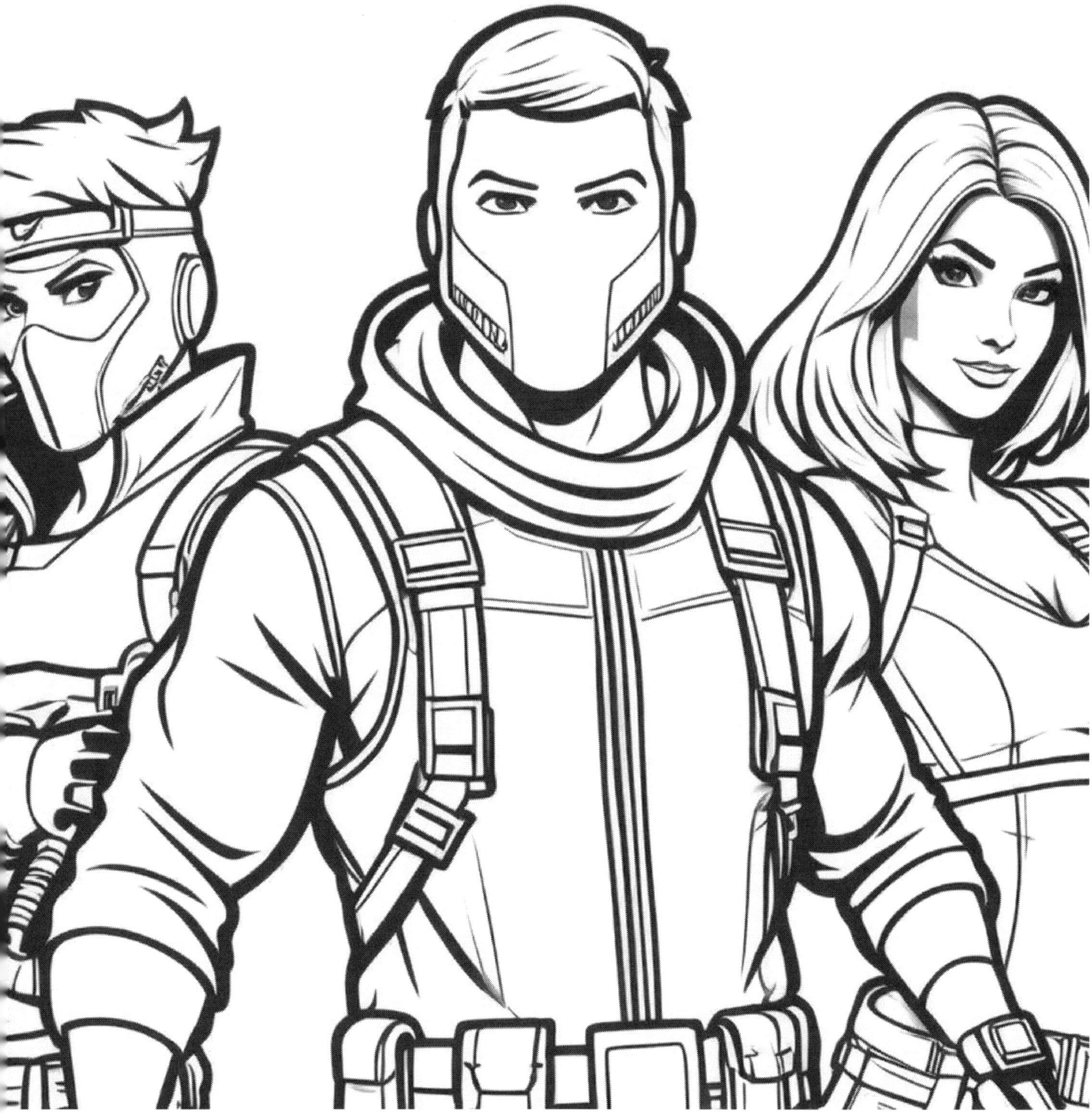

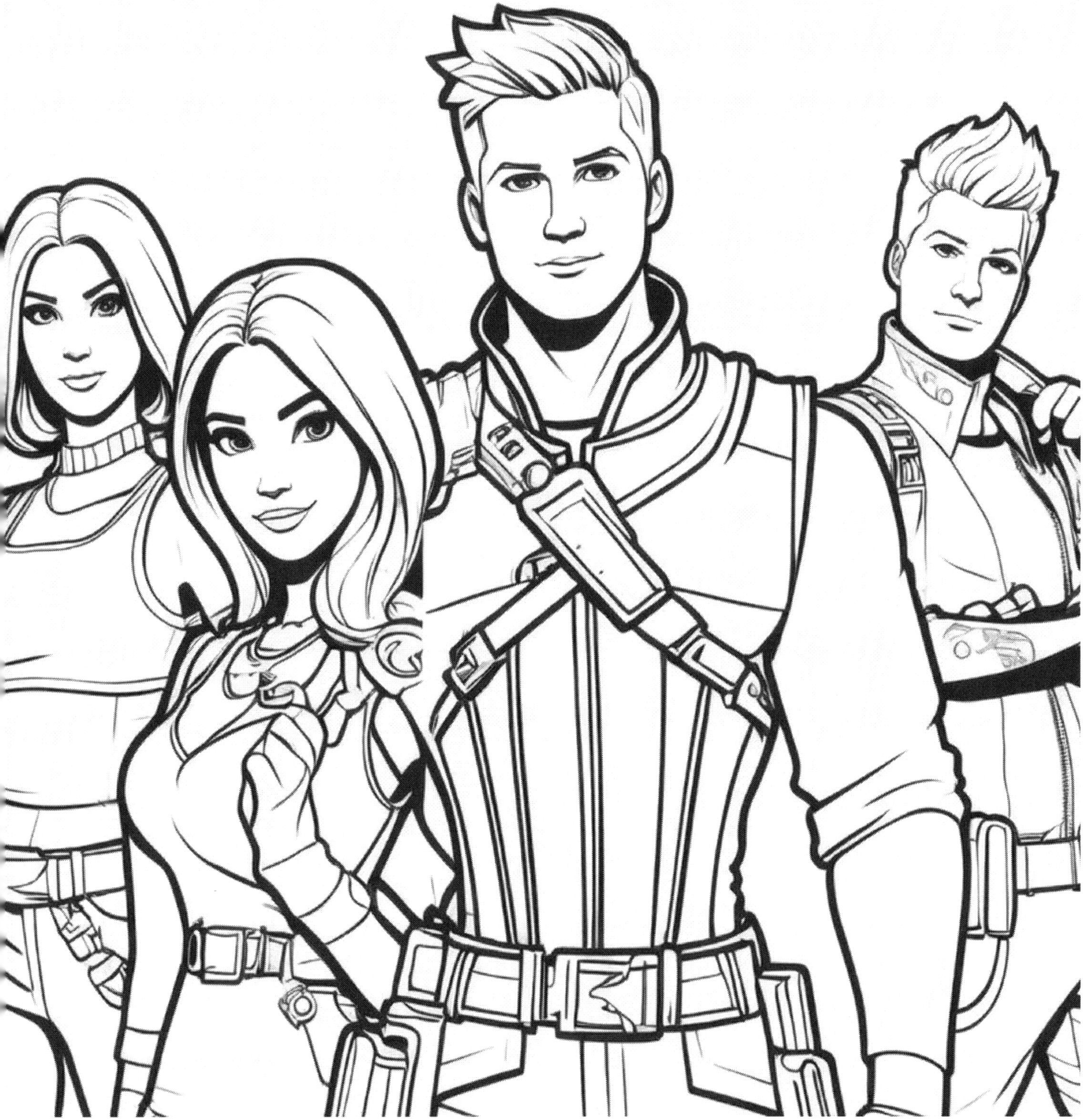

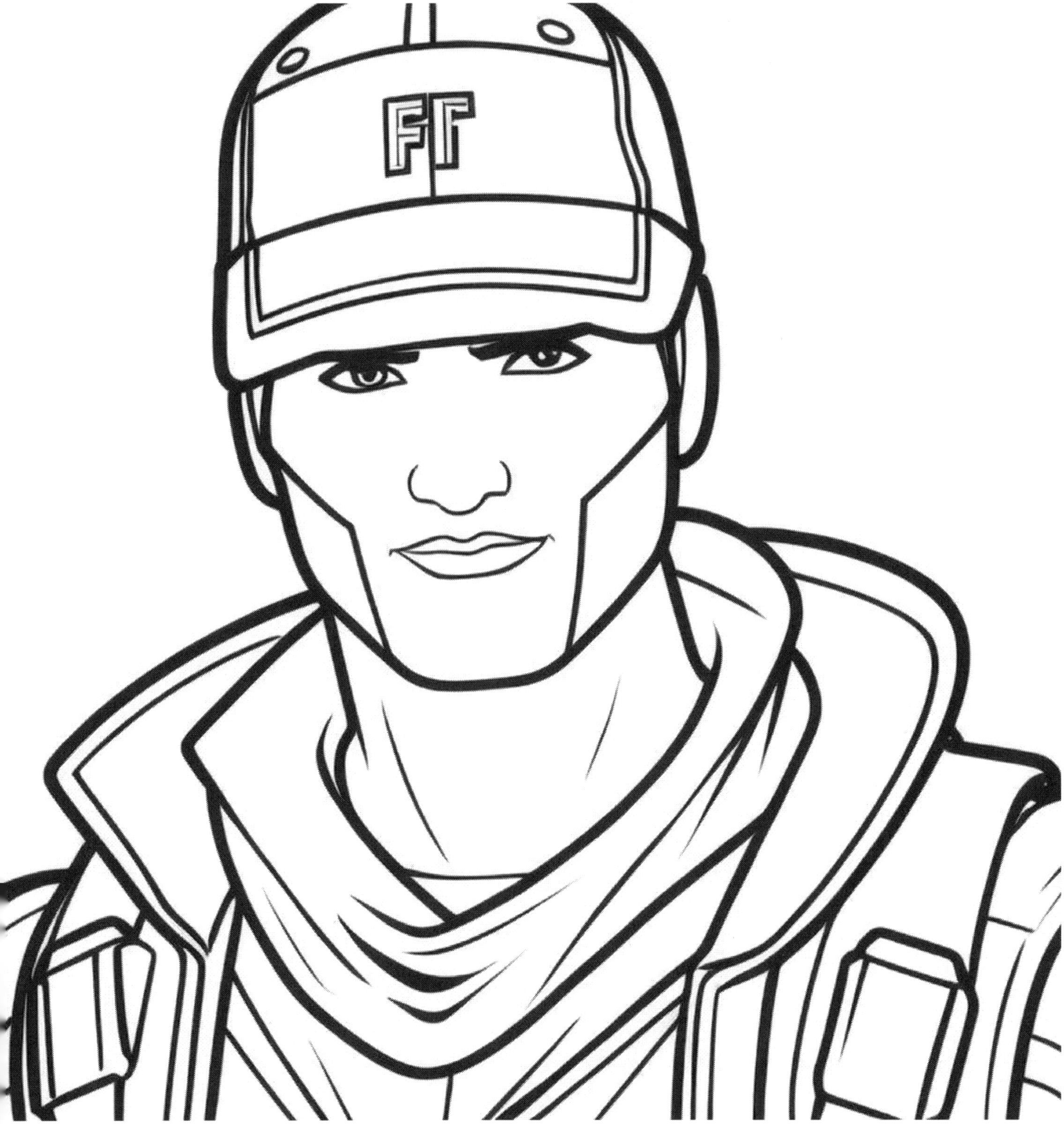
FF

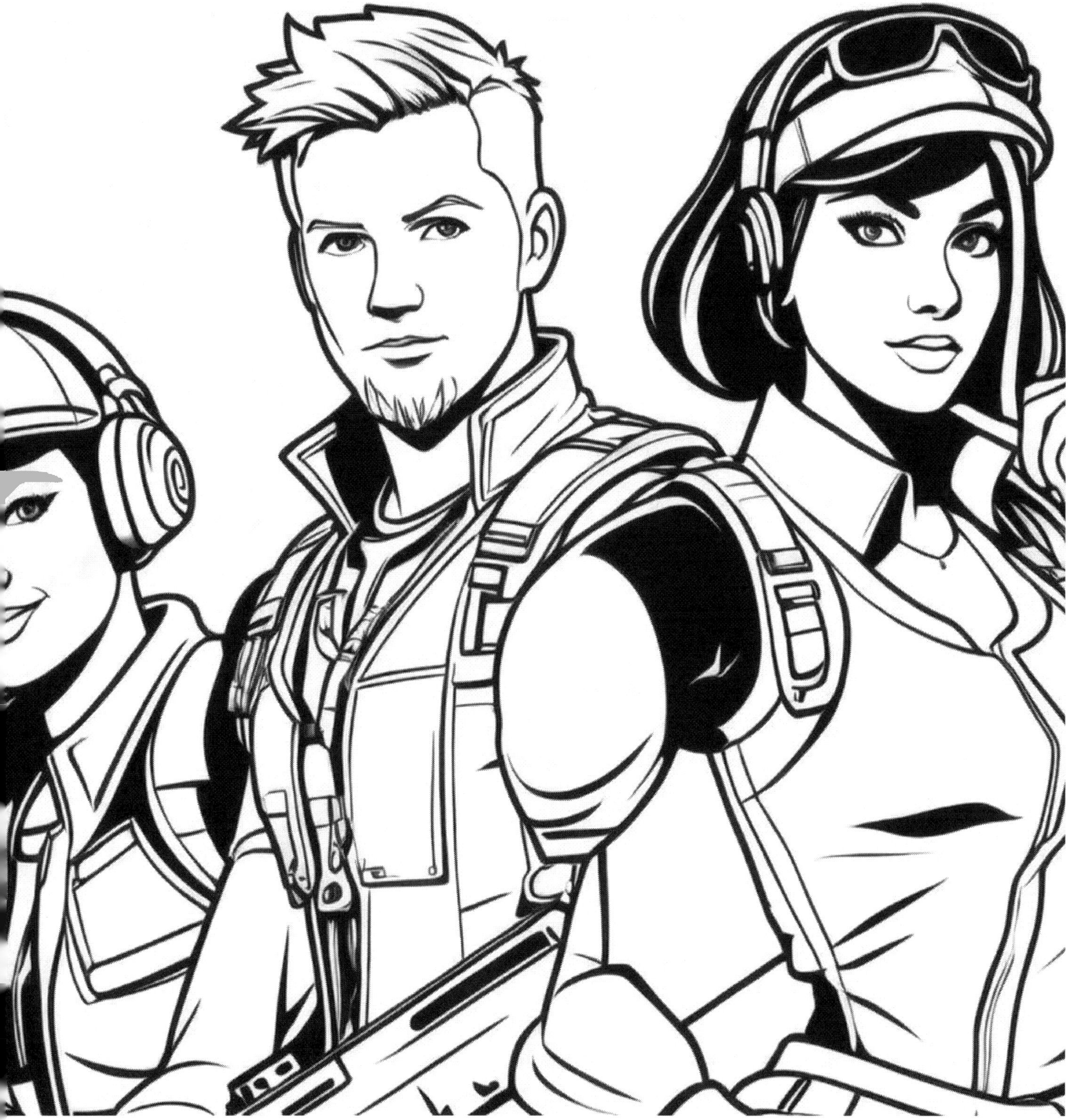

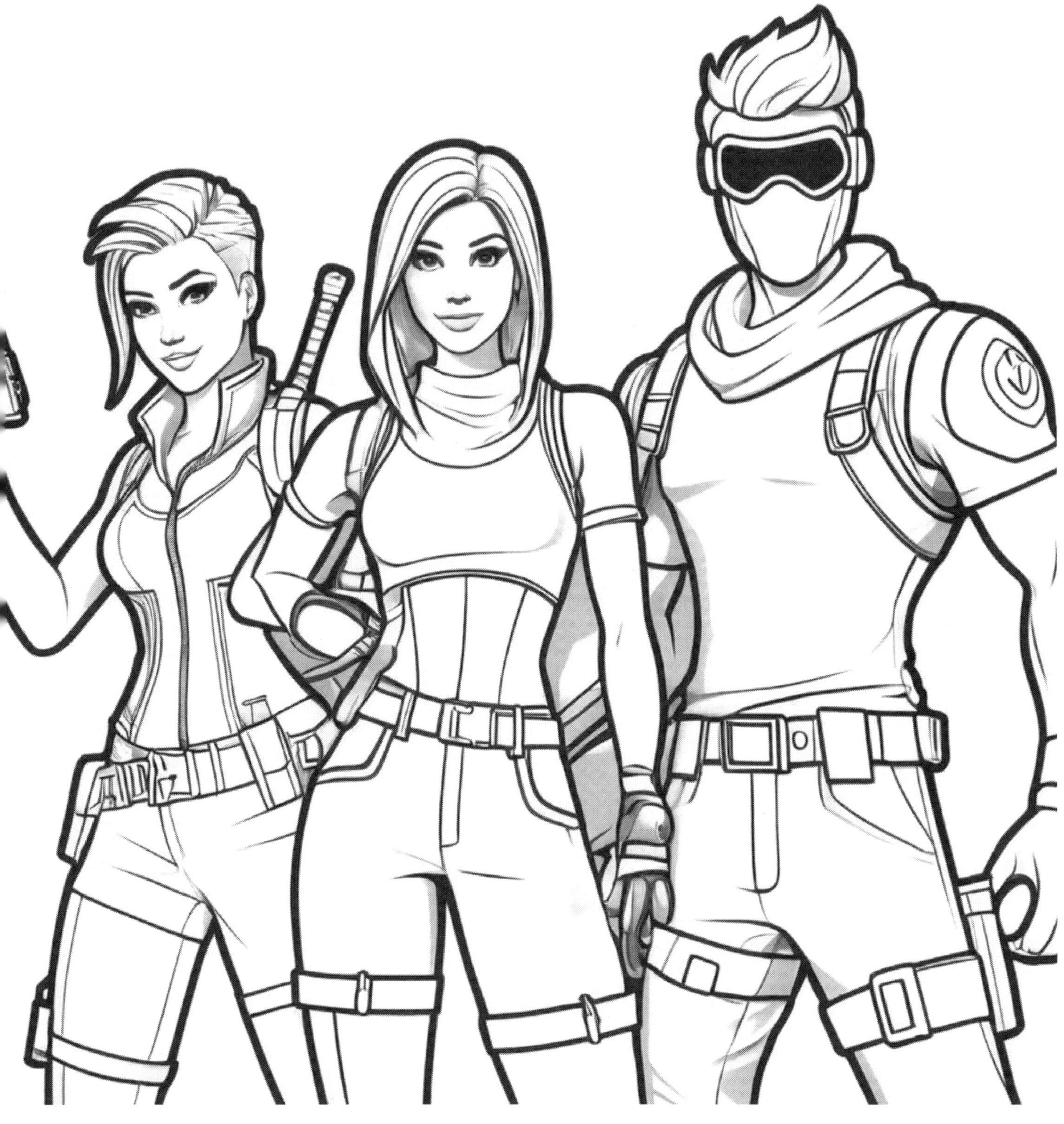

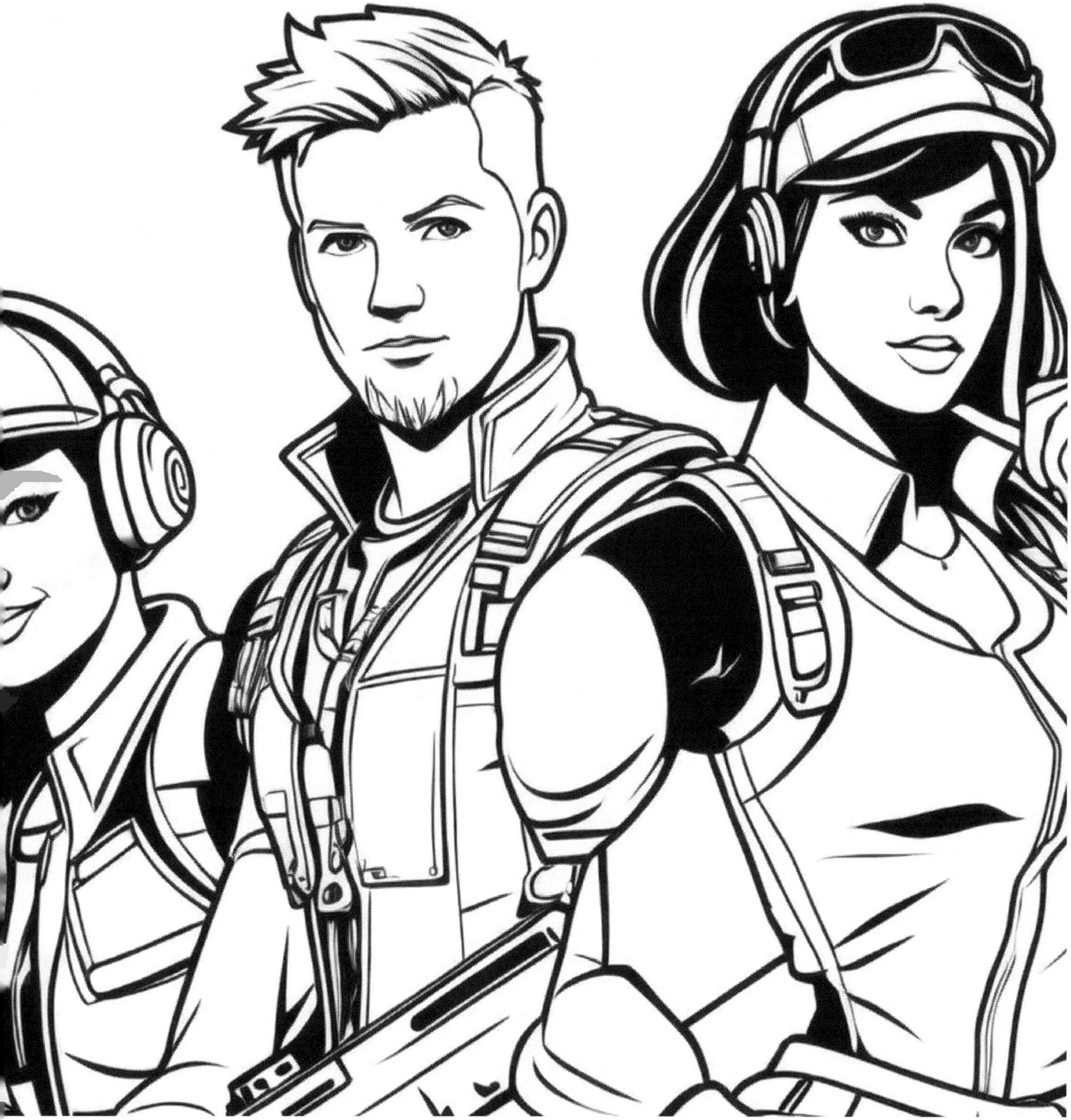

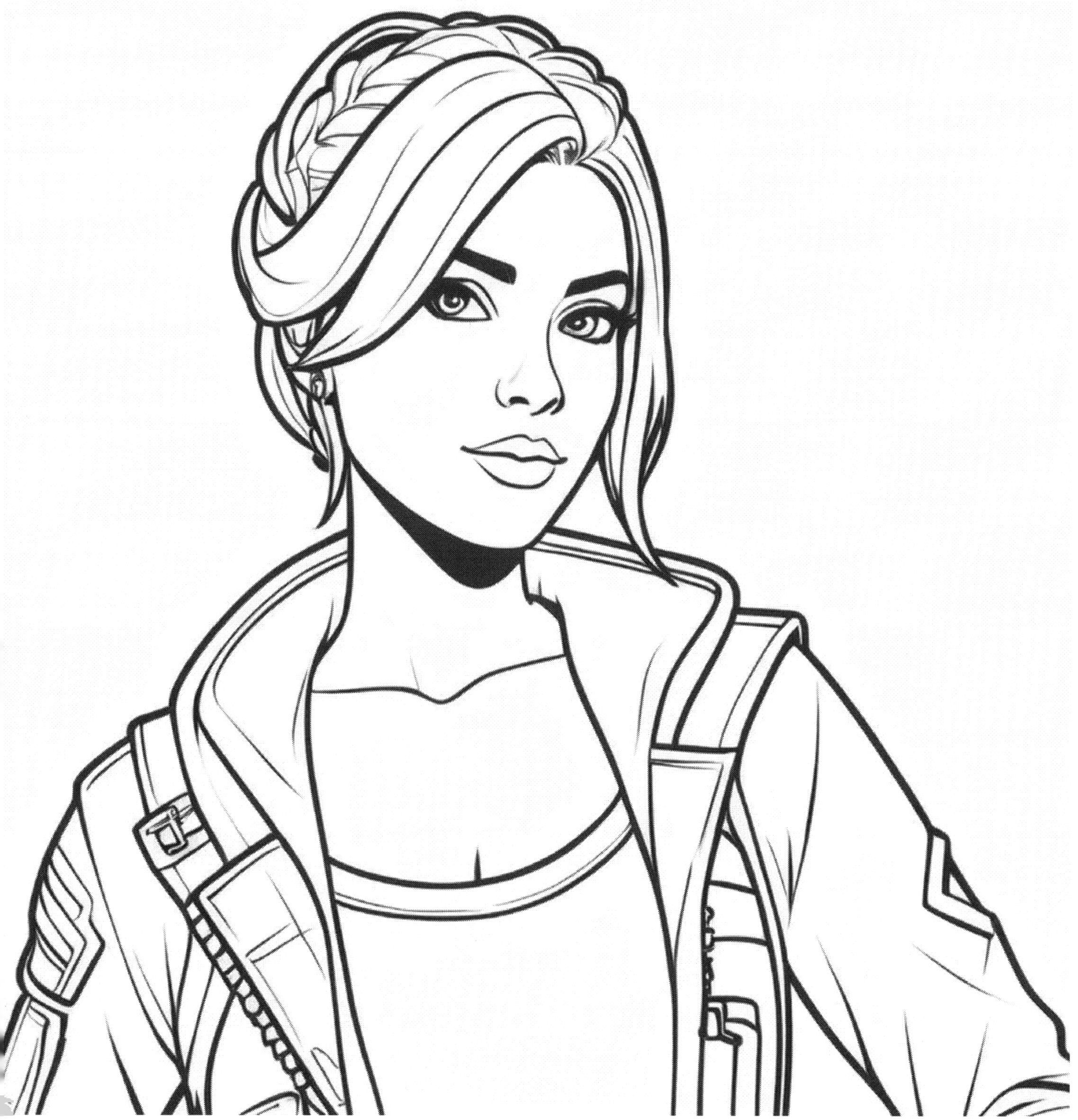

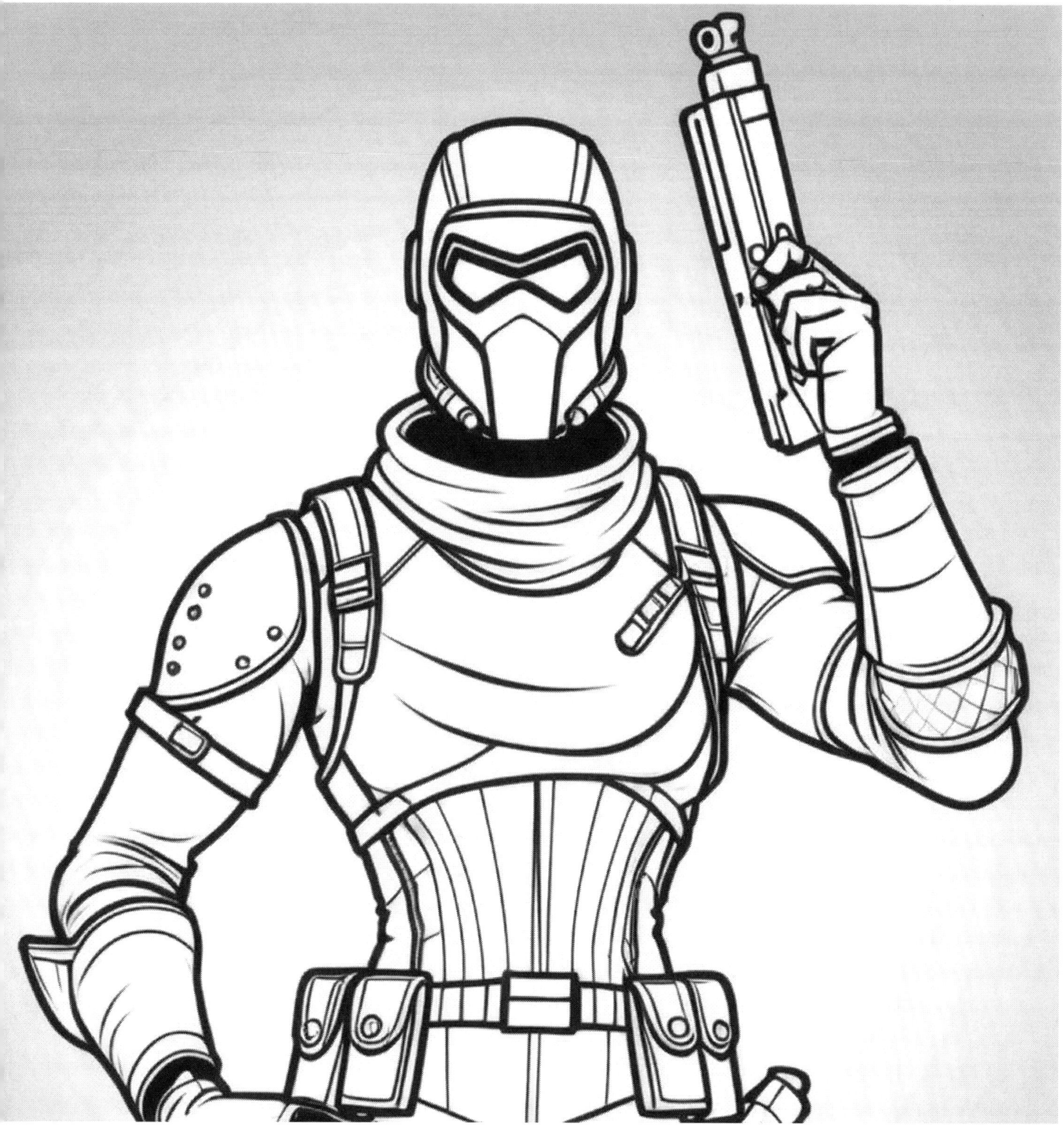

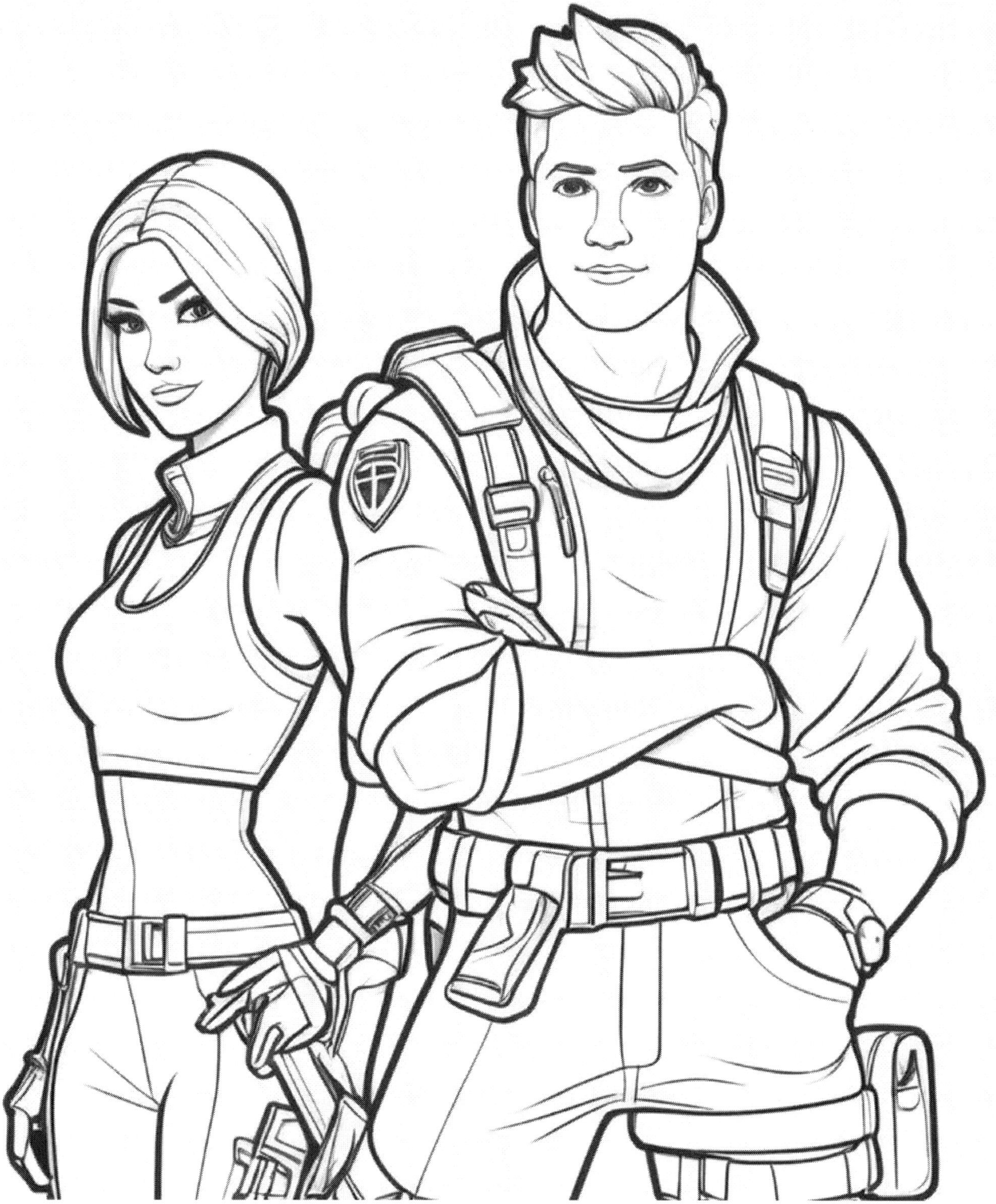

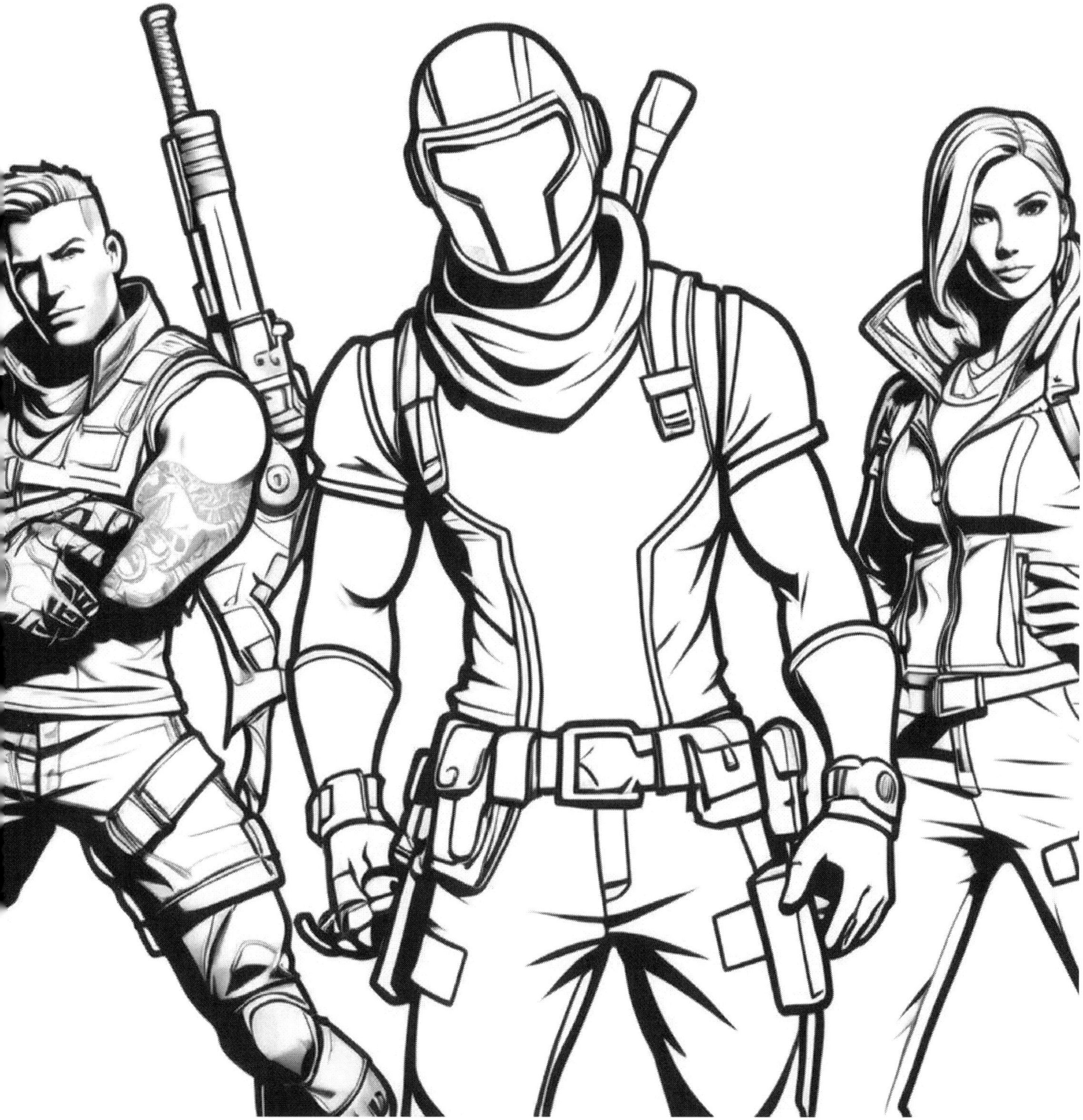

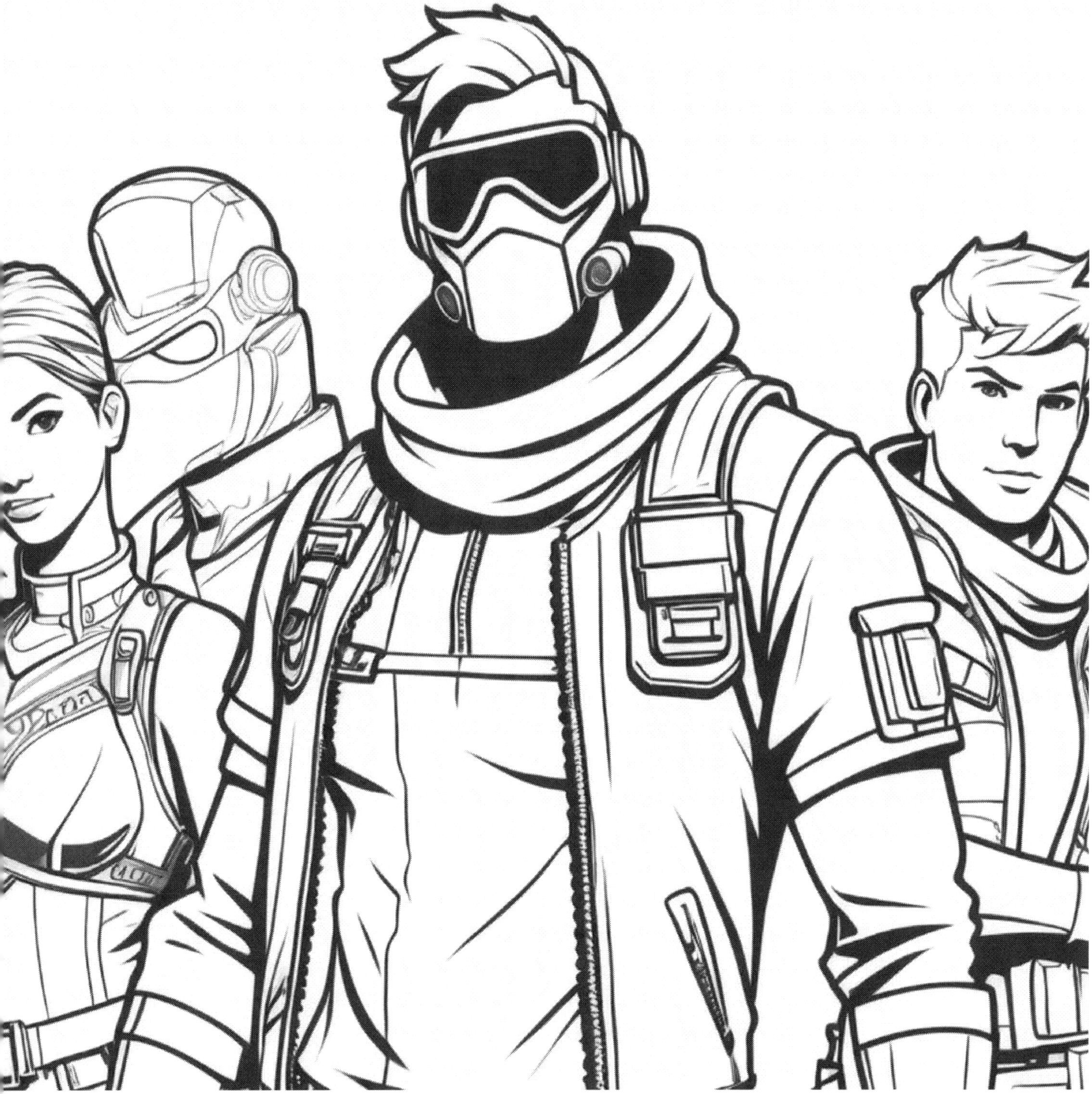

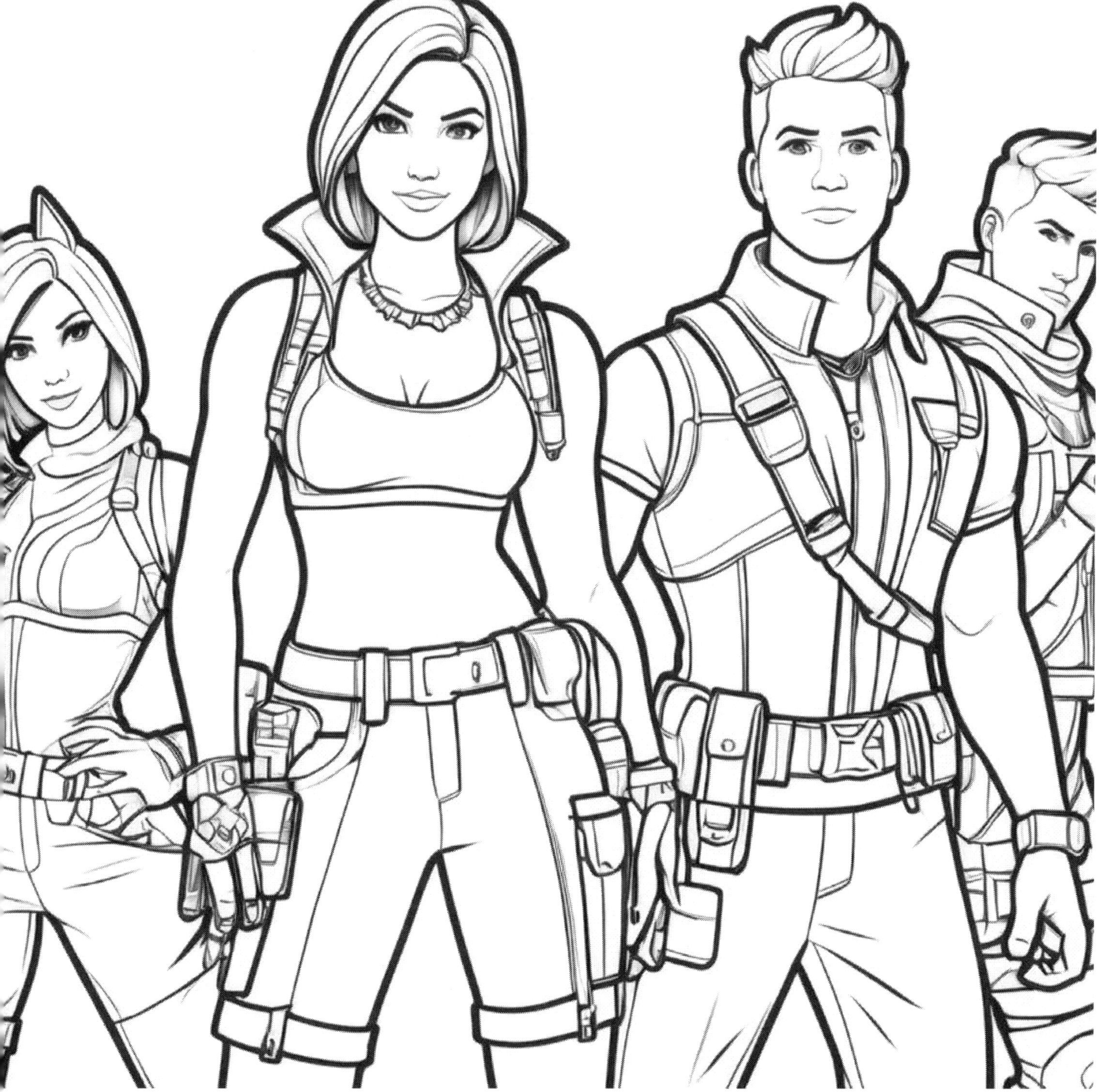

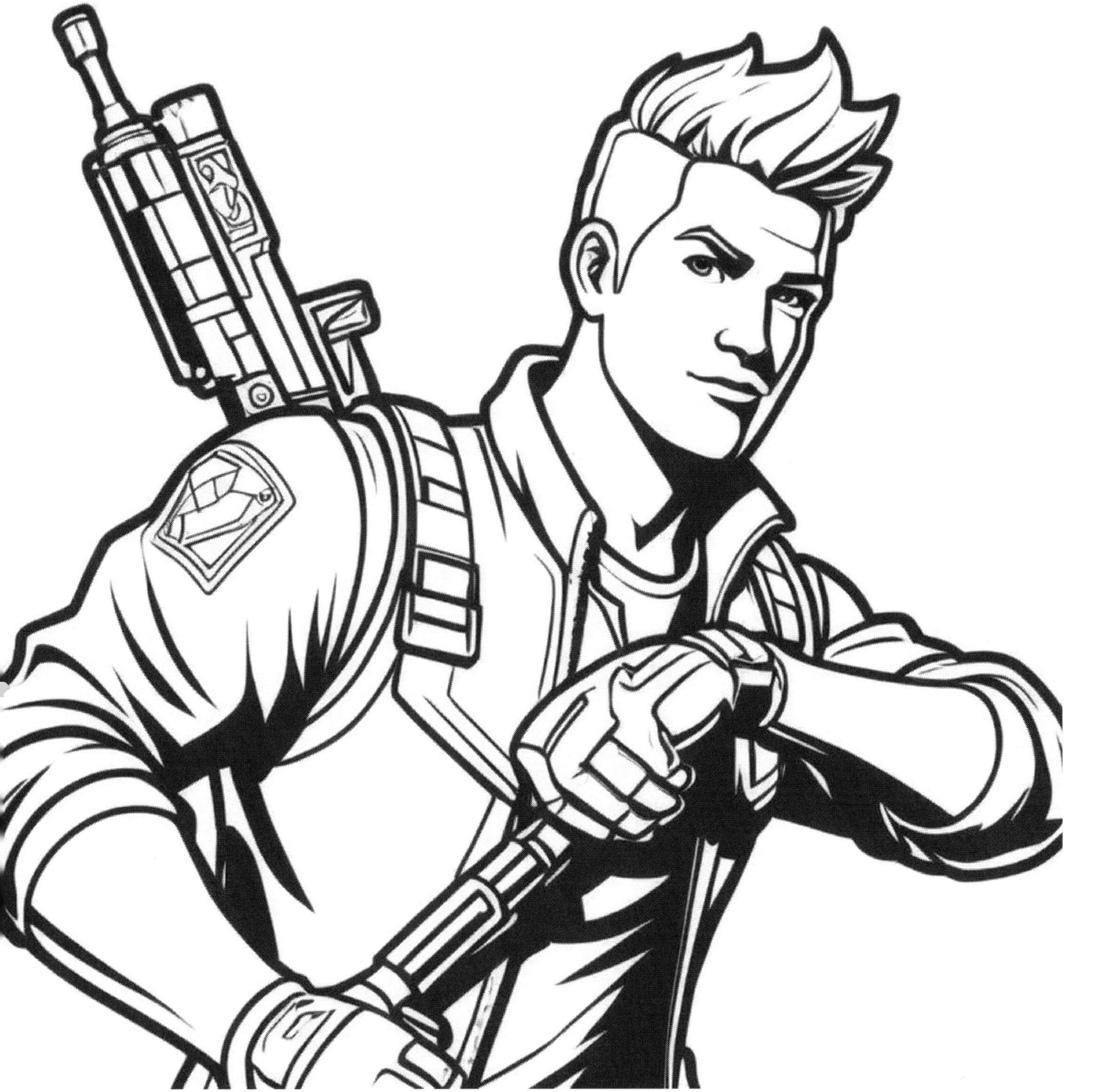

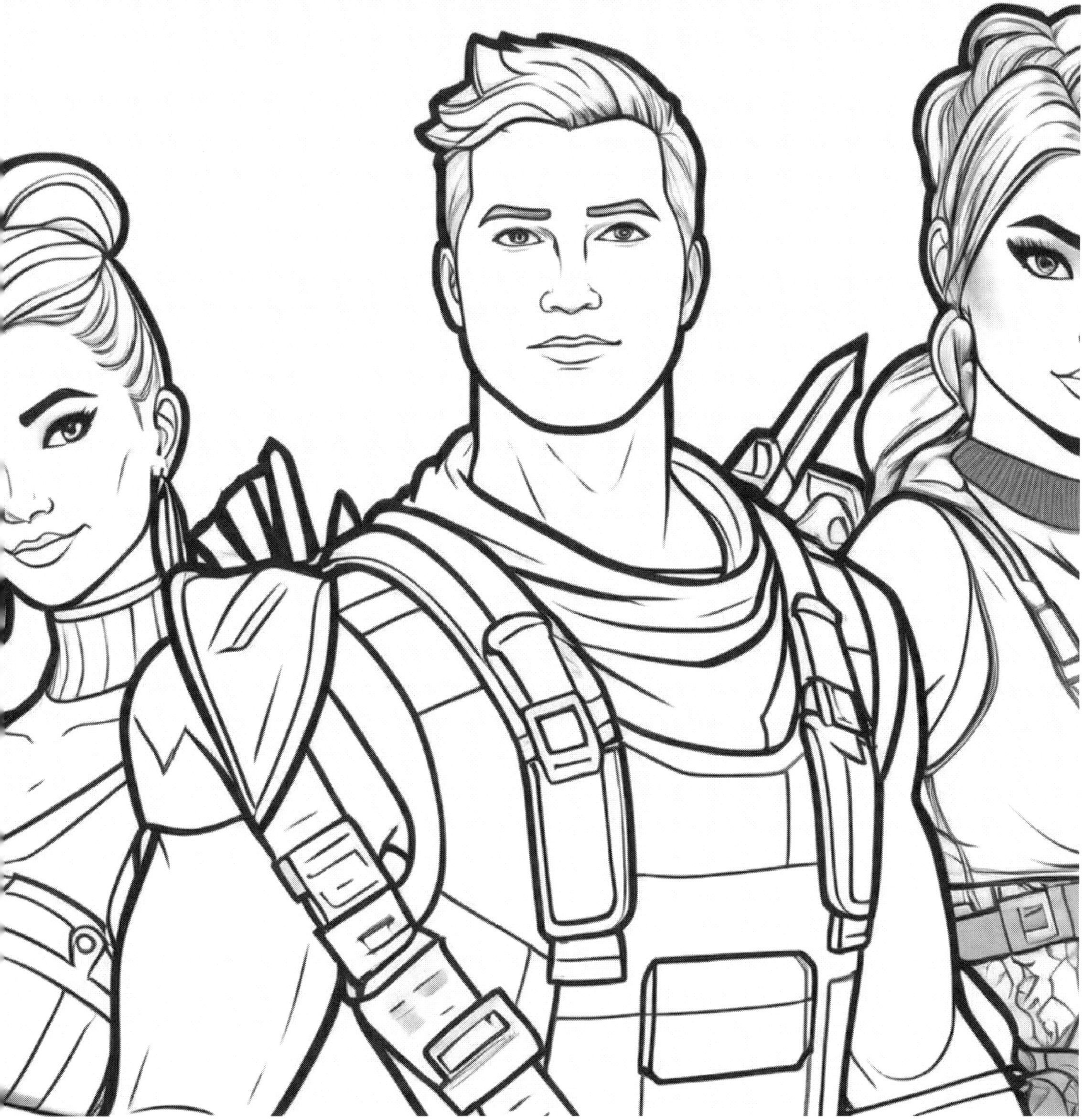

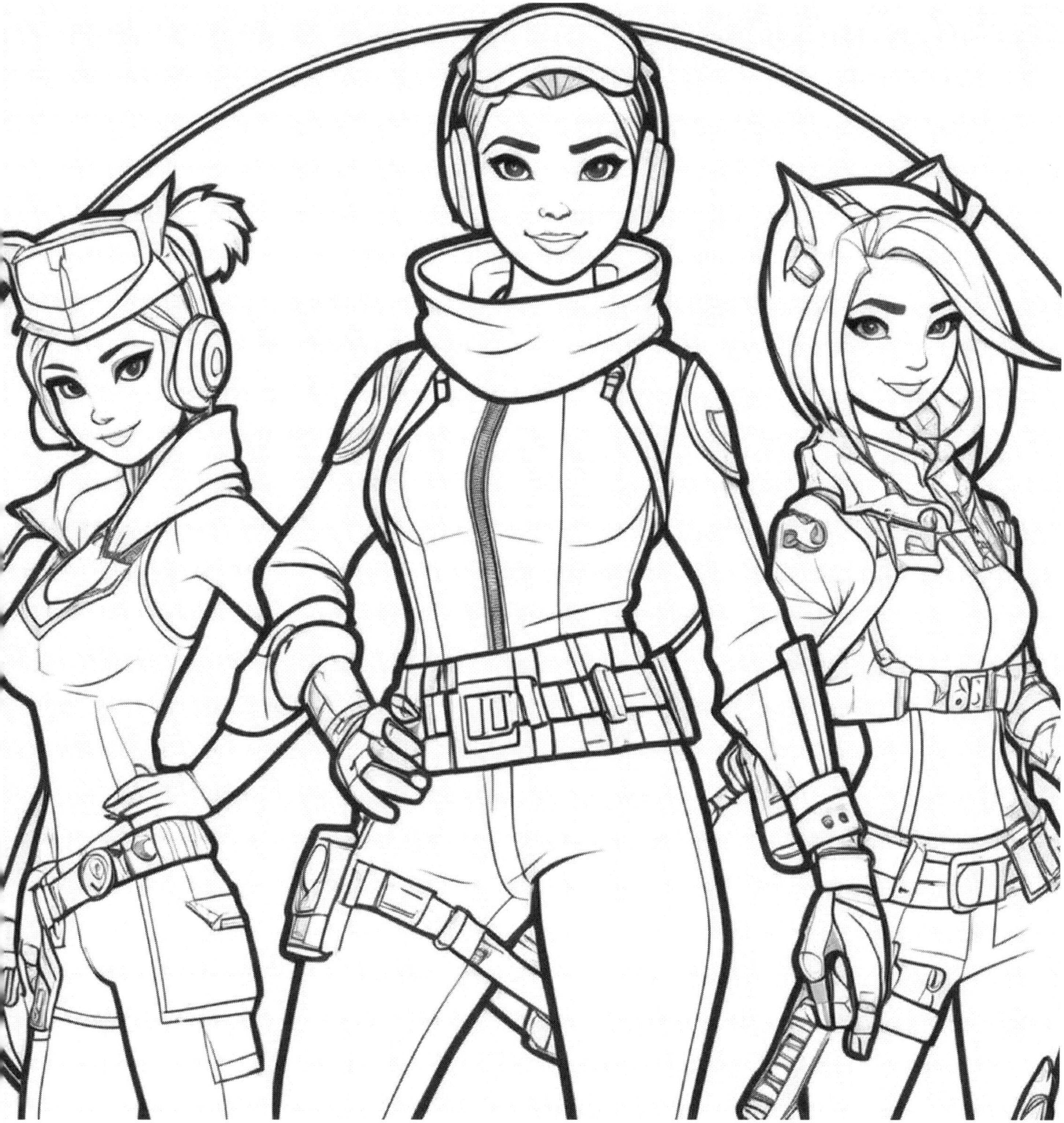

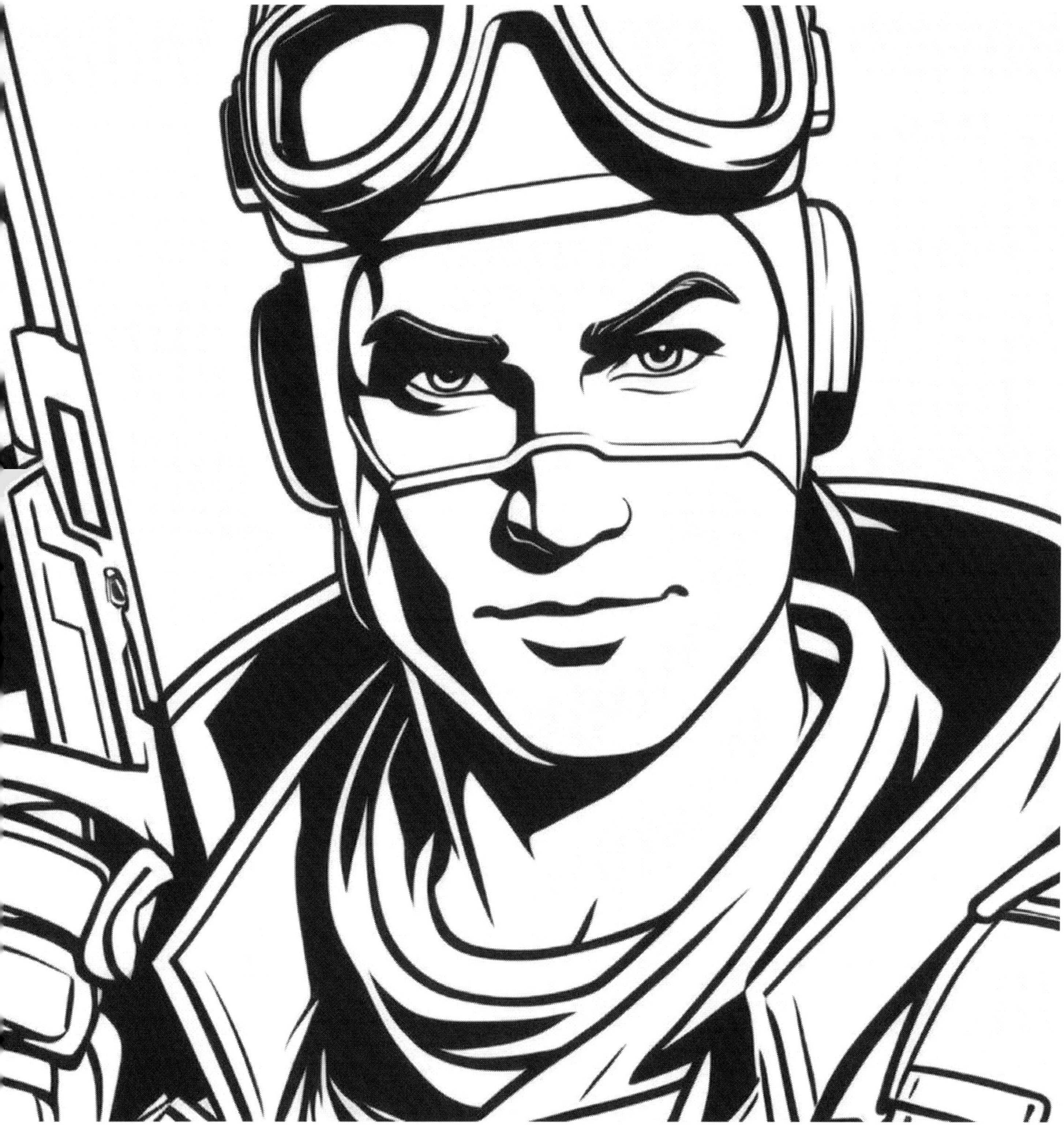

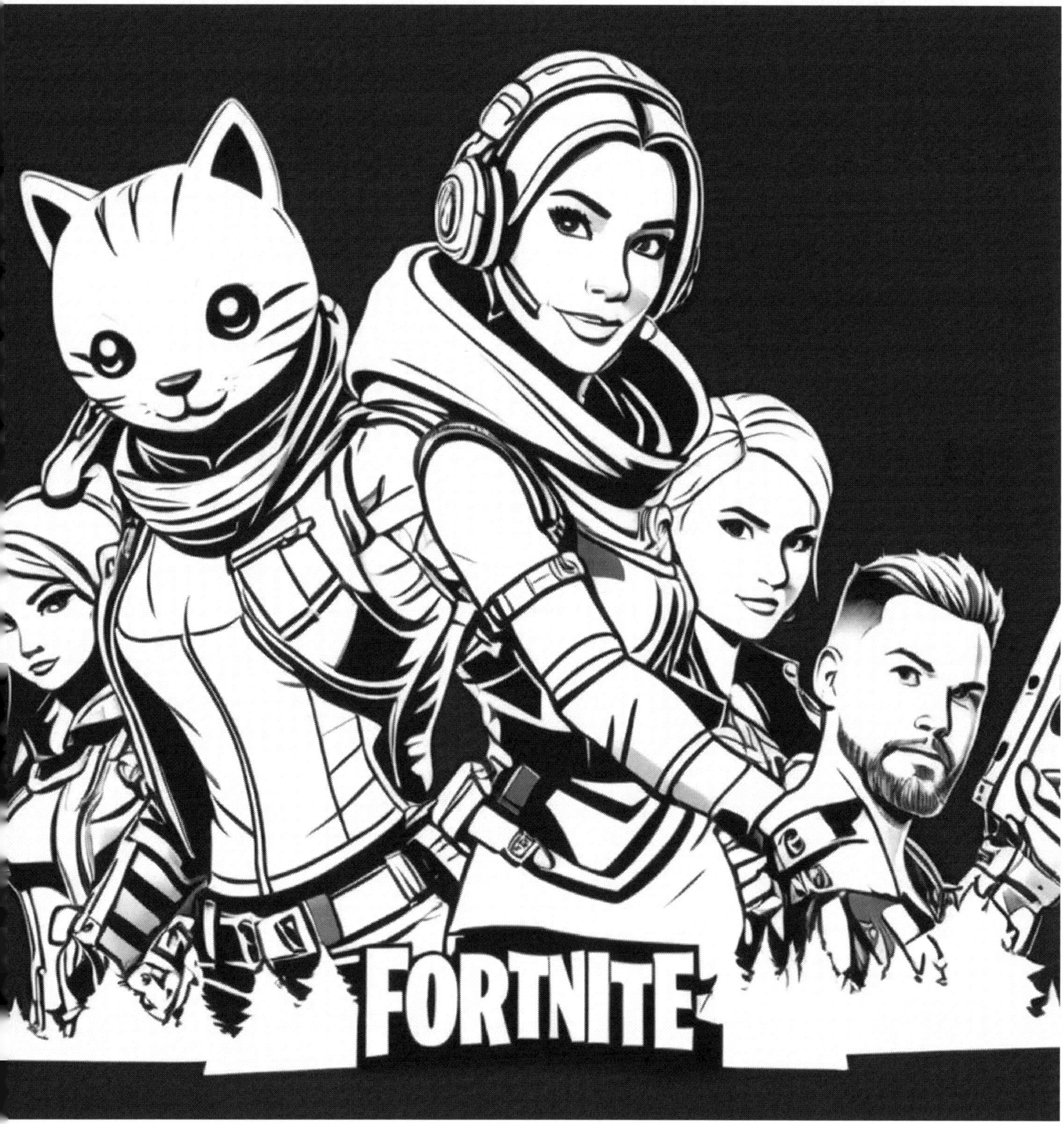
FORTNITE

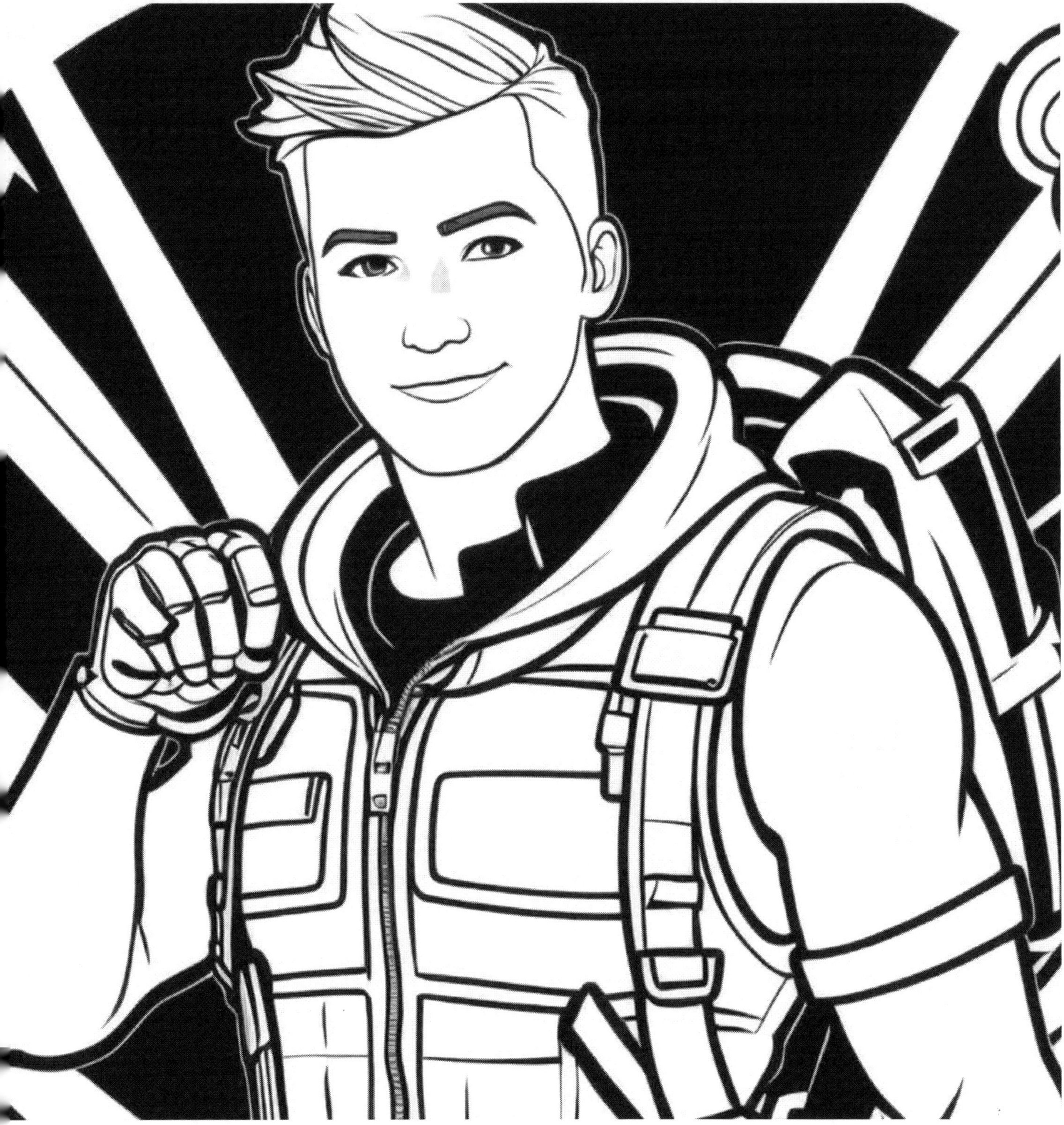

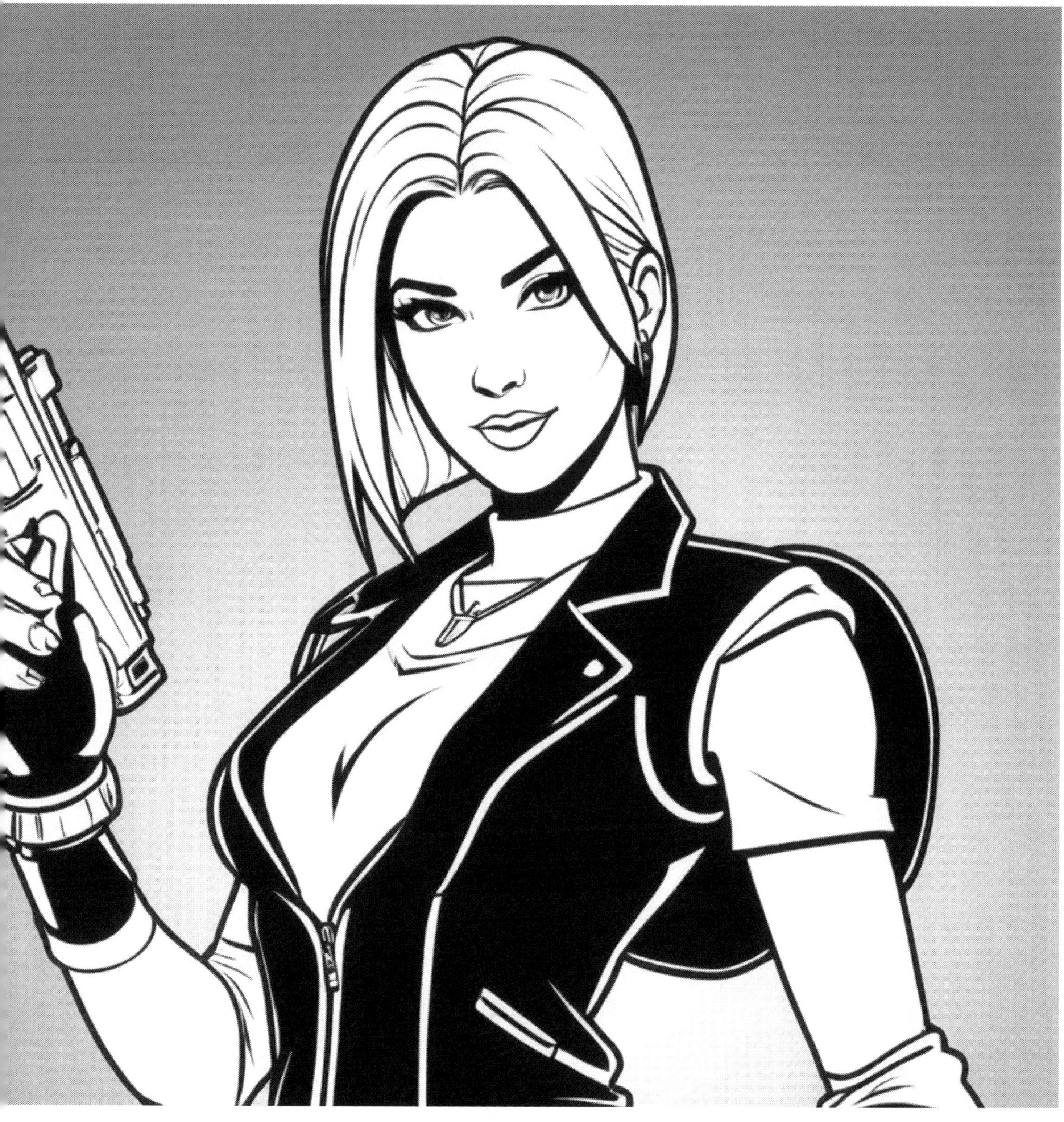

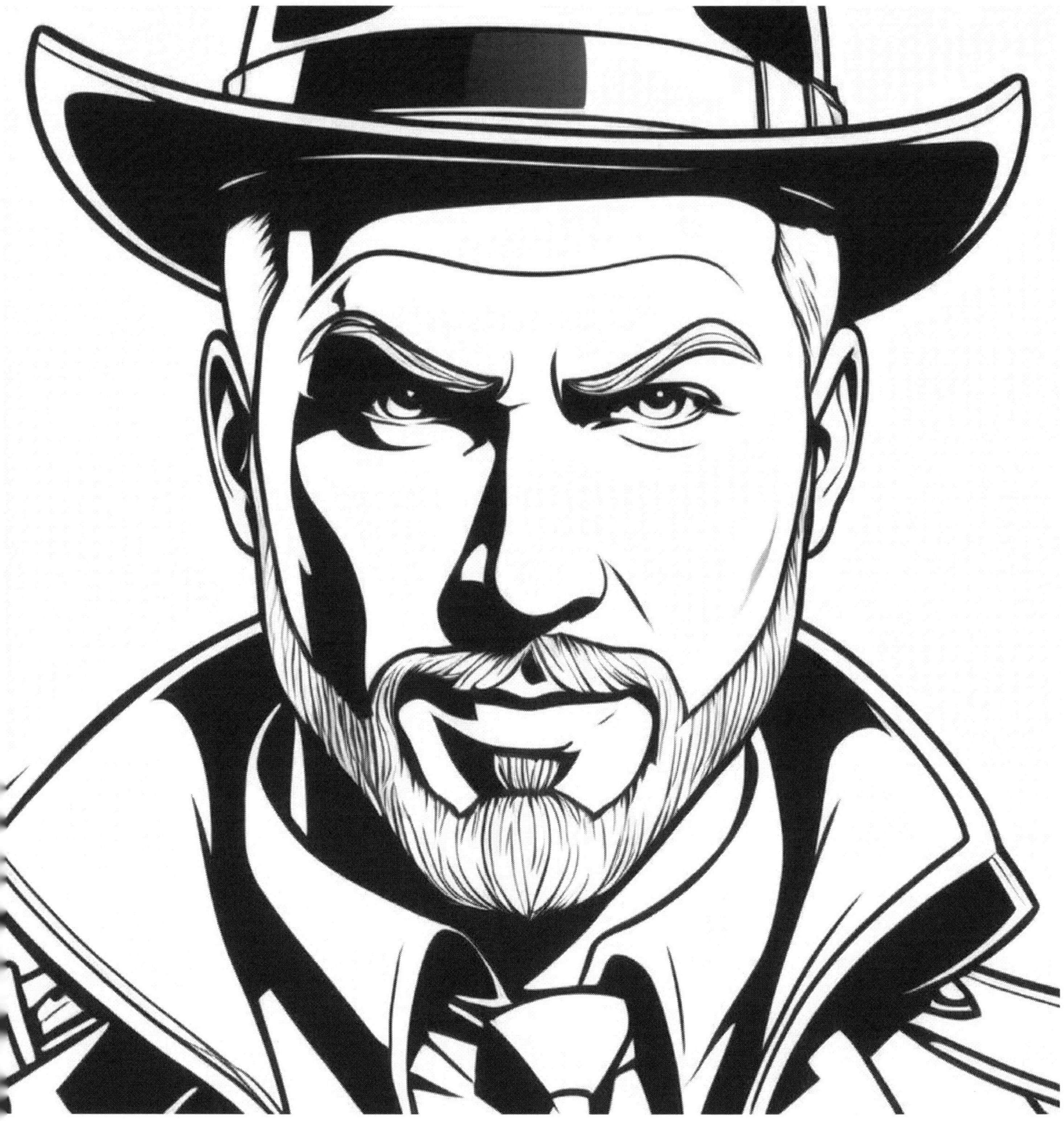

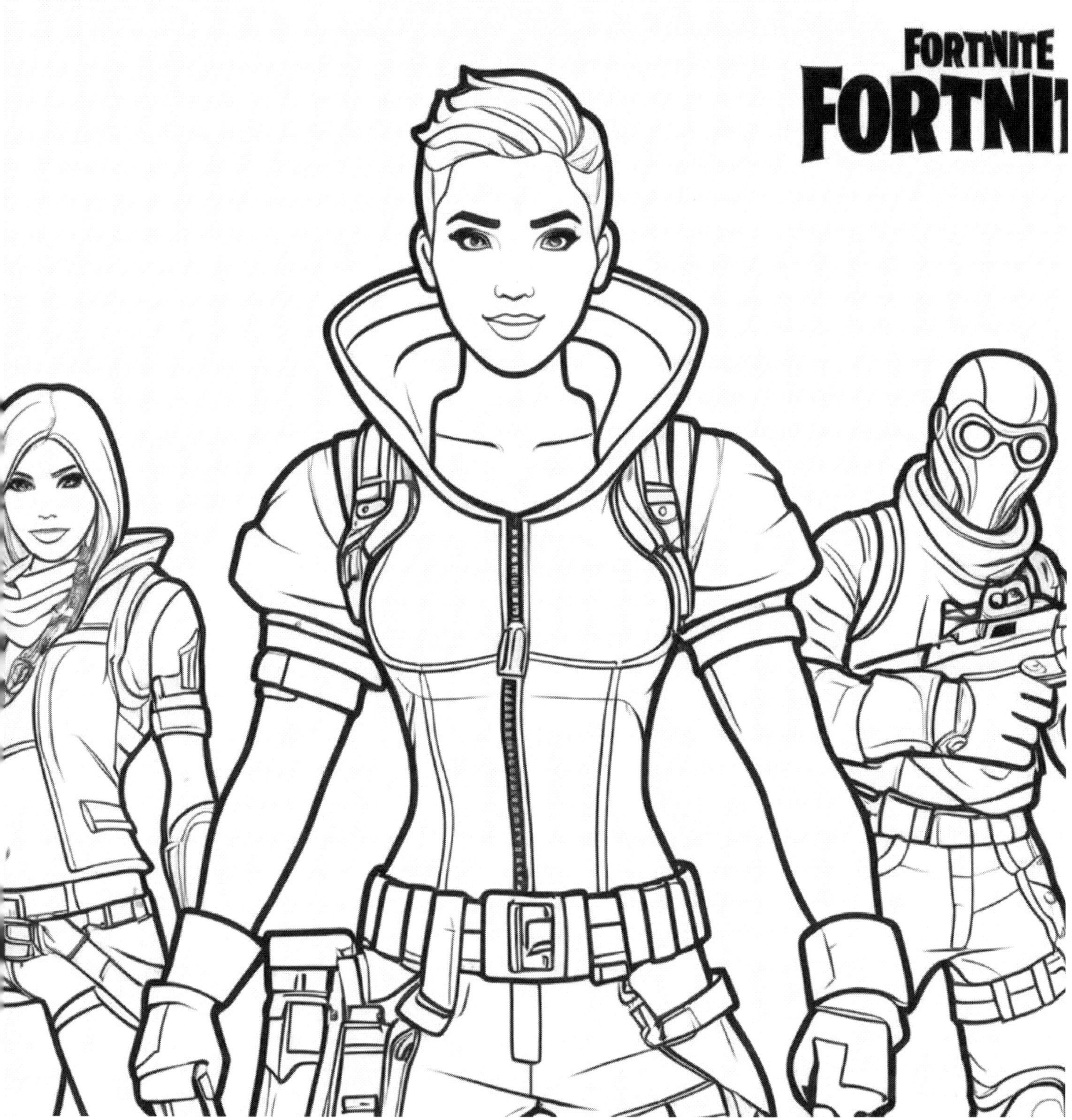
FORTNITE
FORTNIT

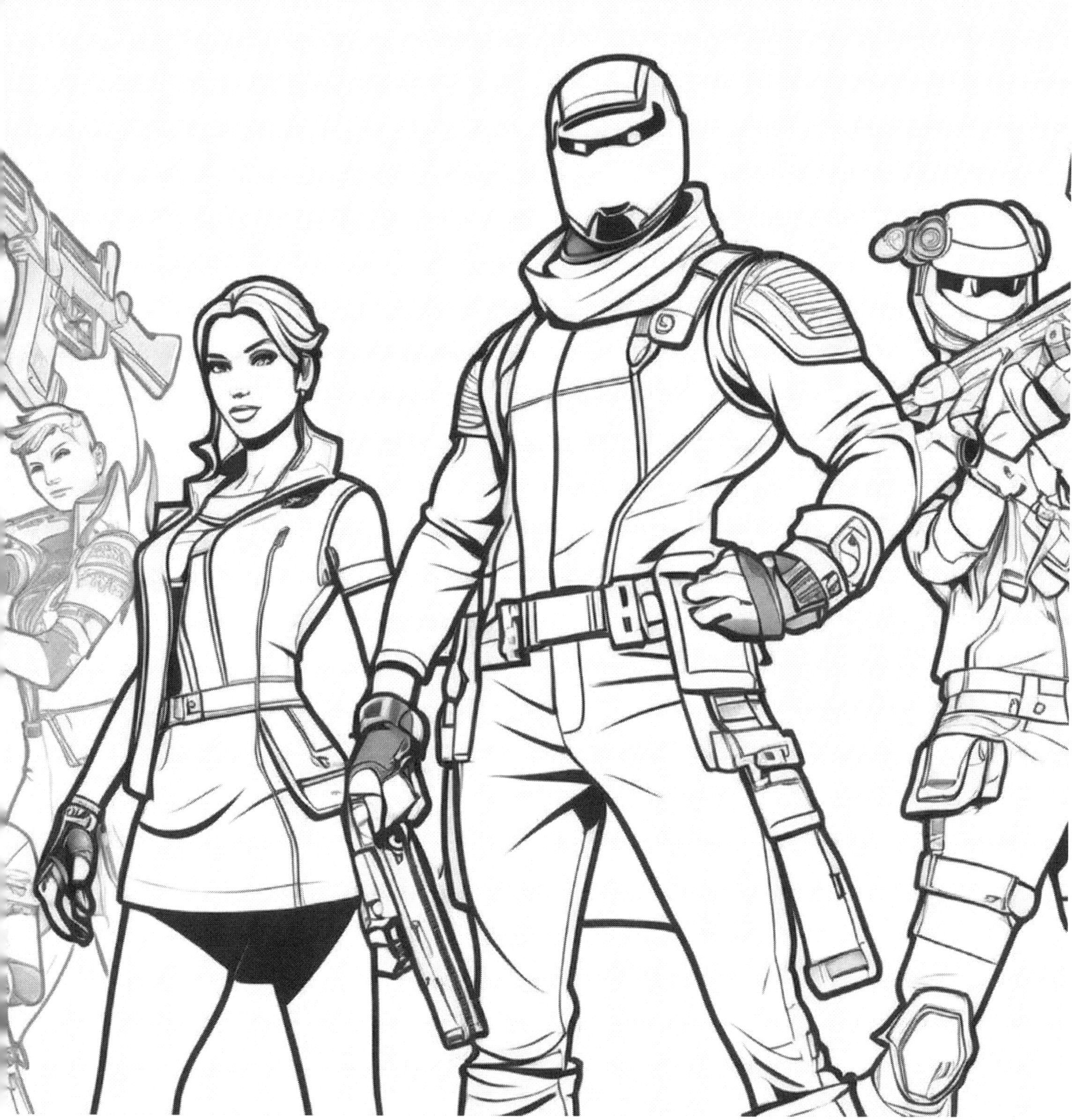

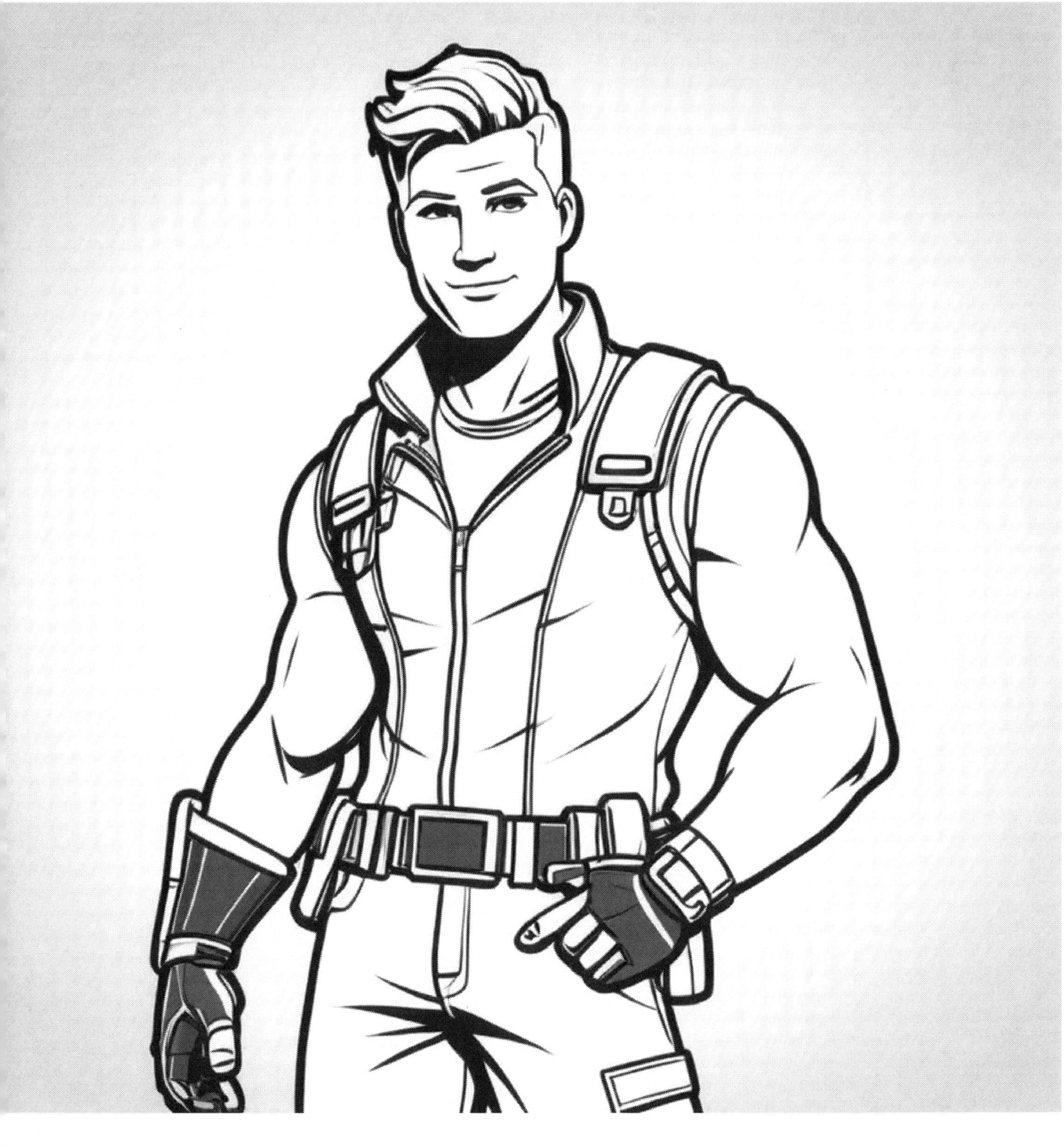

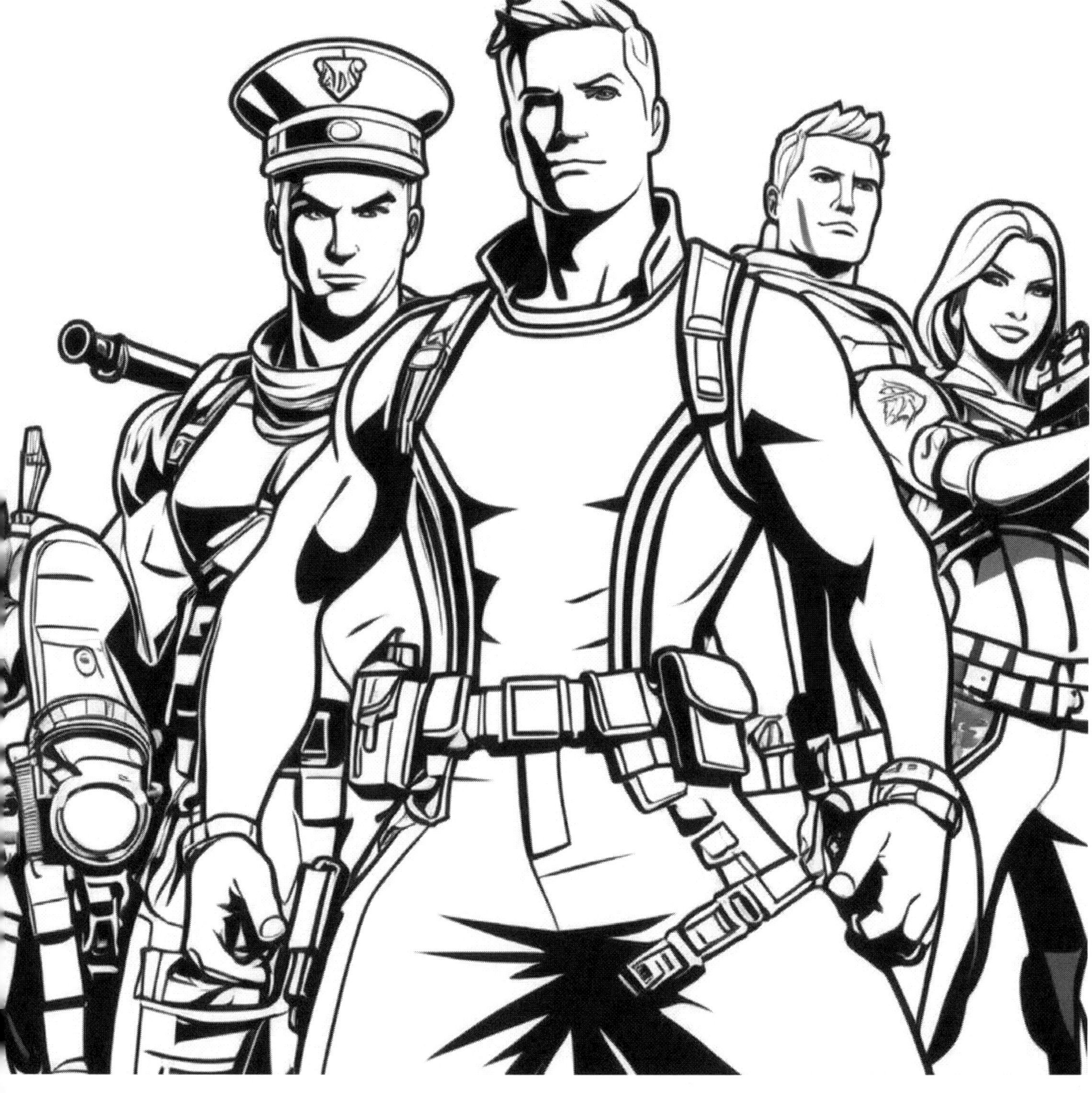

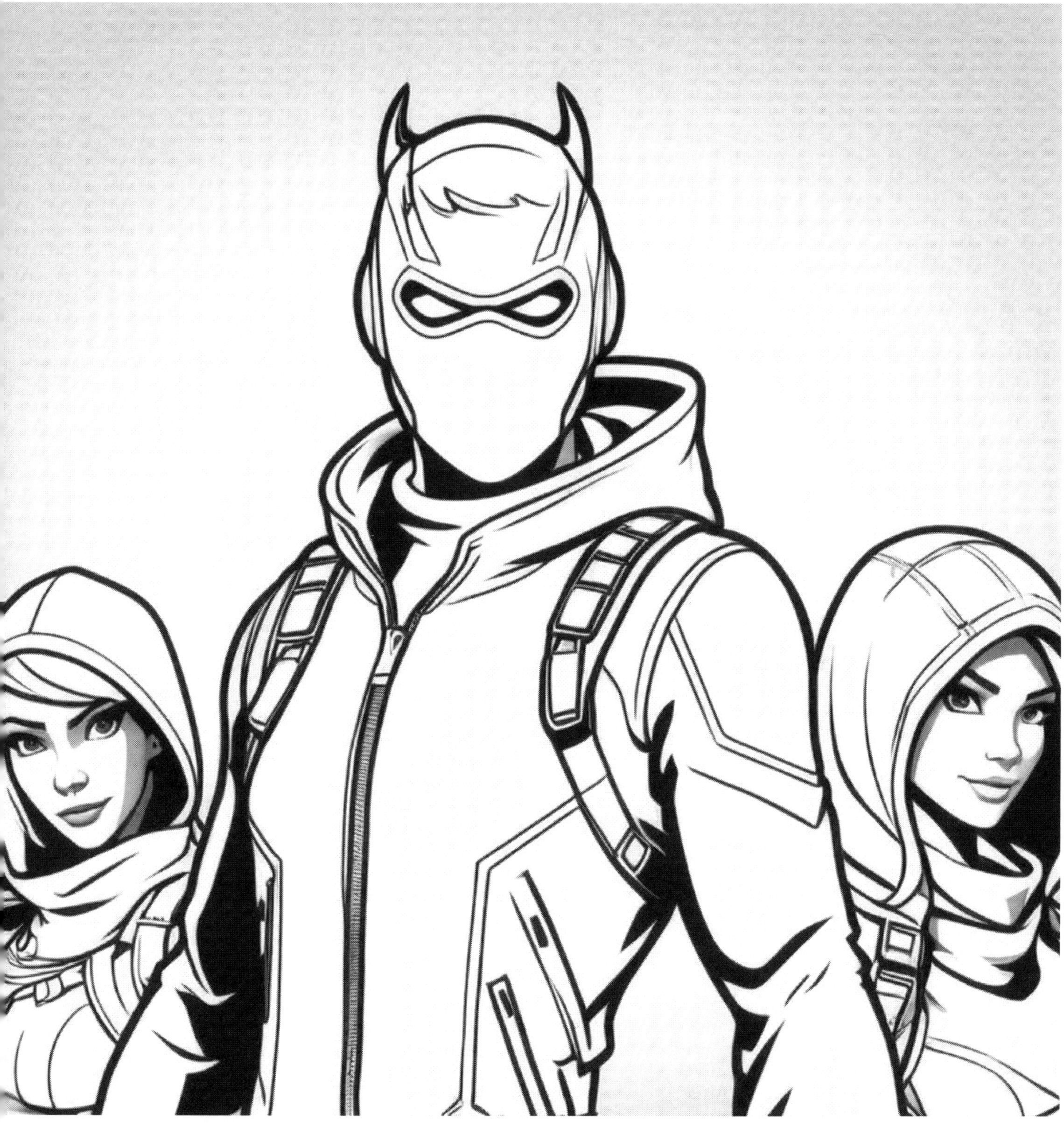

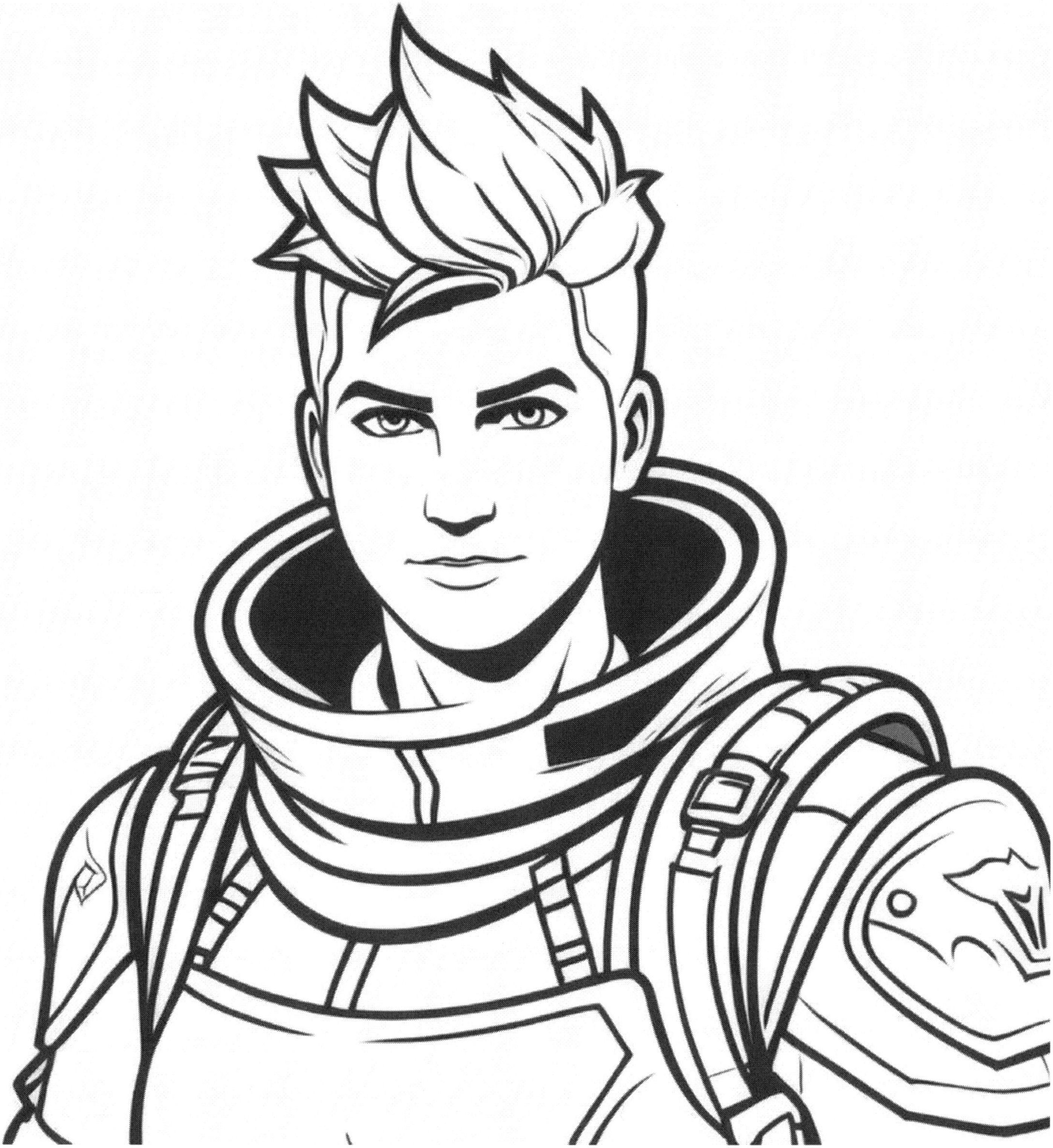

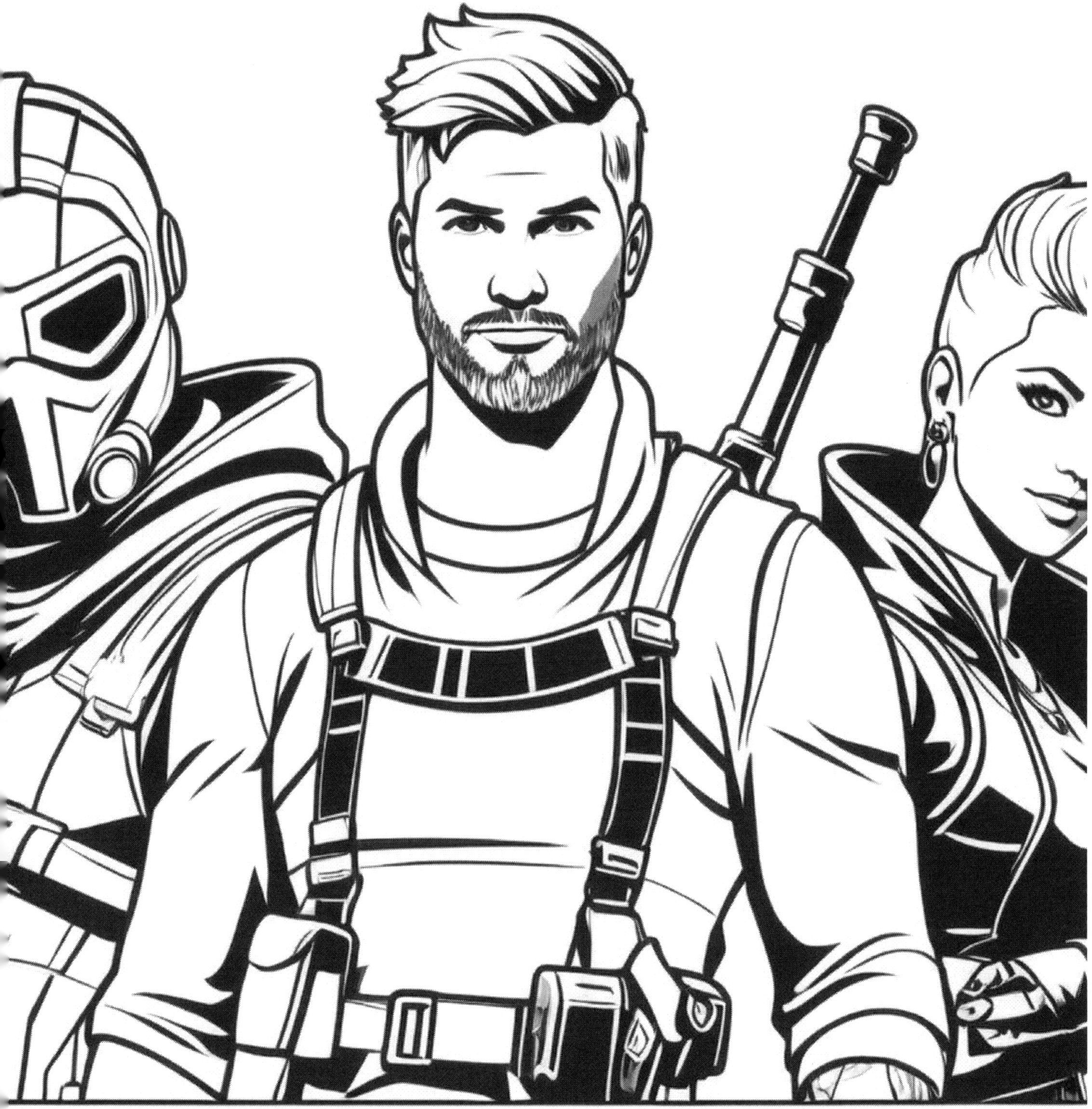

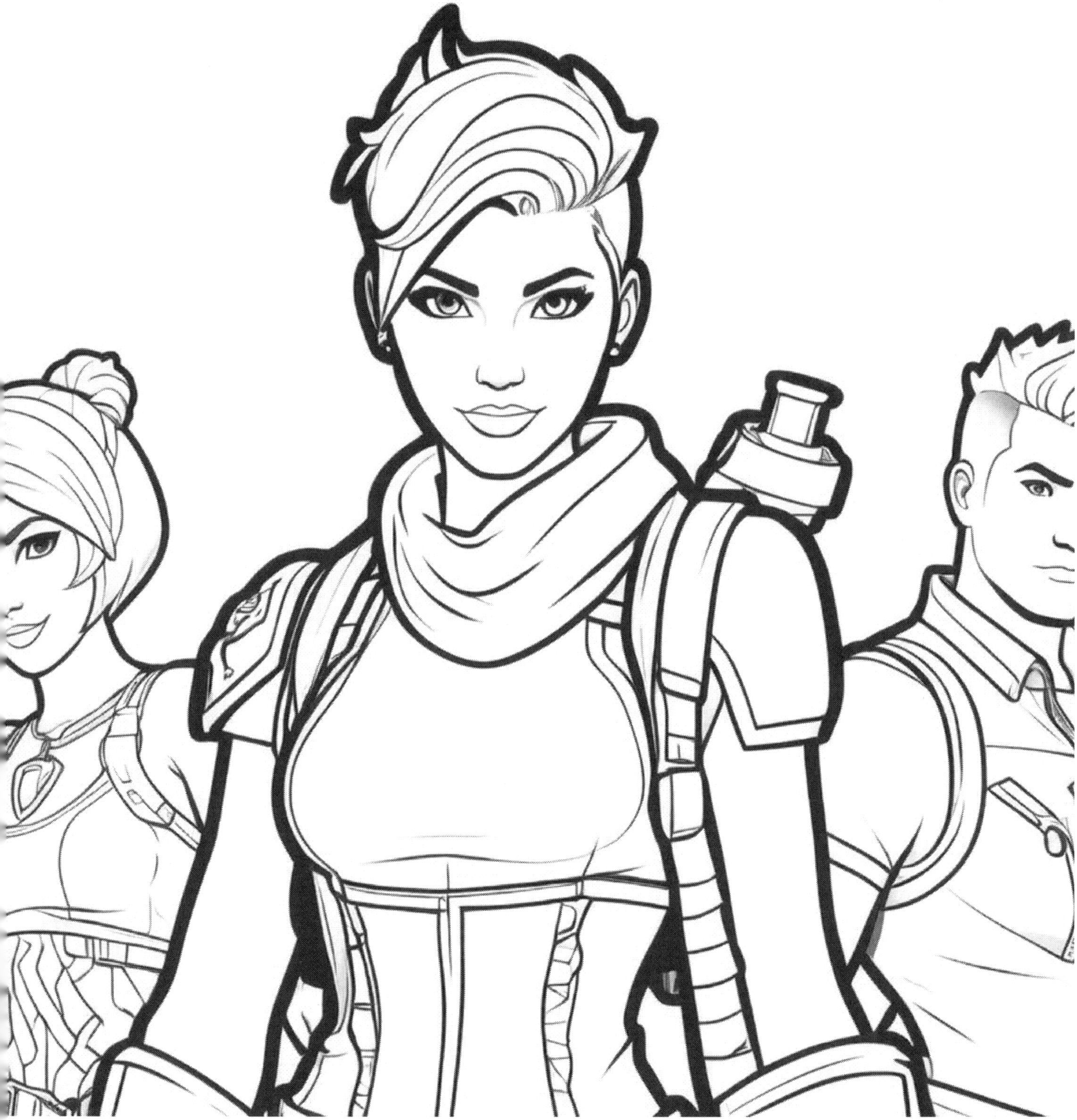

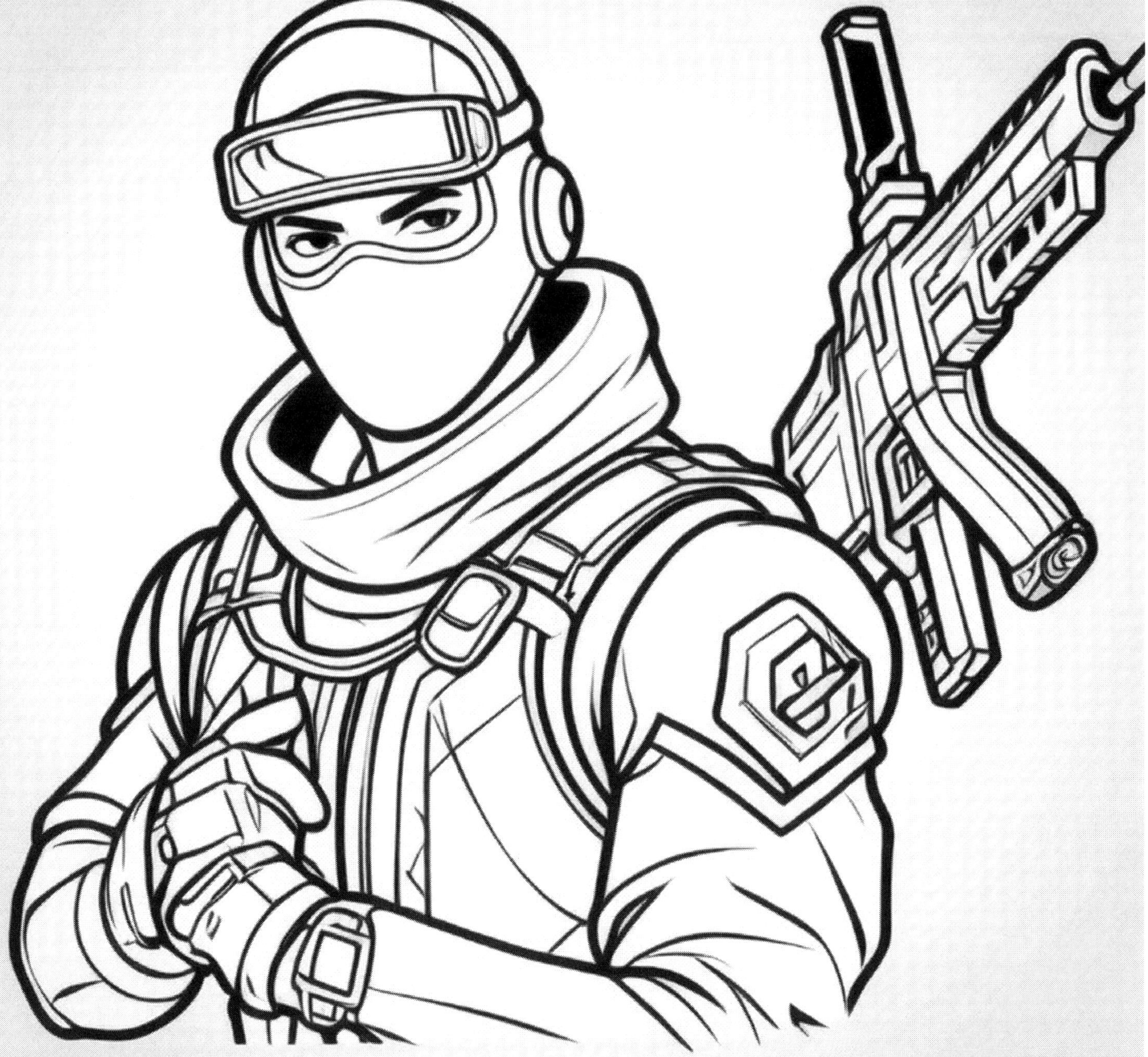

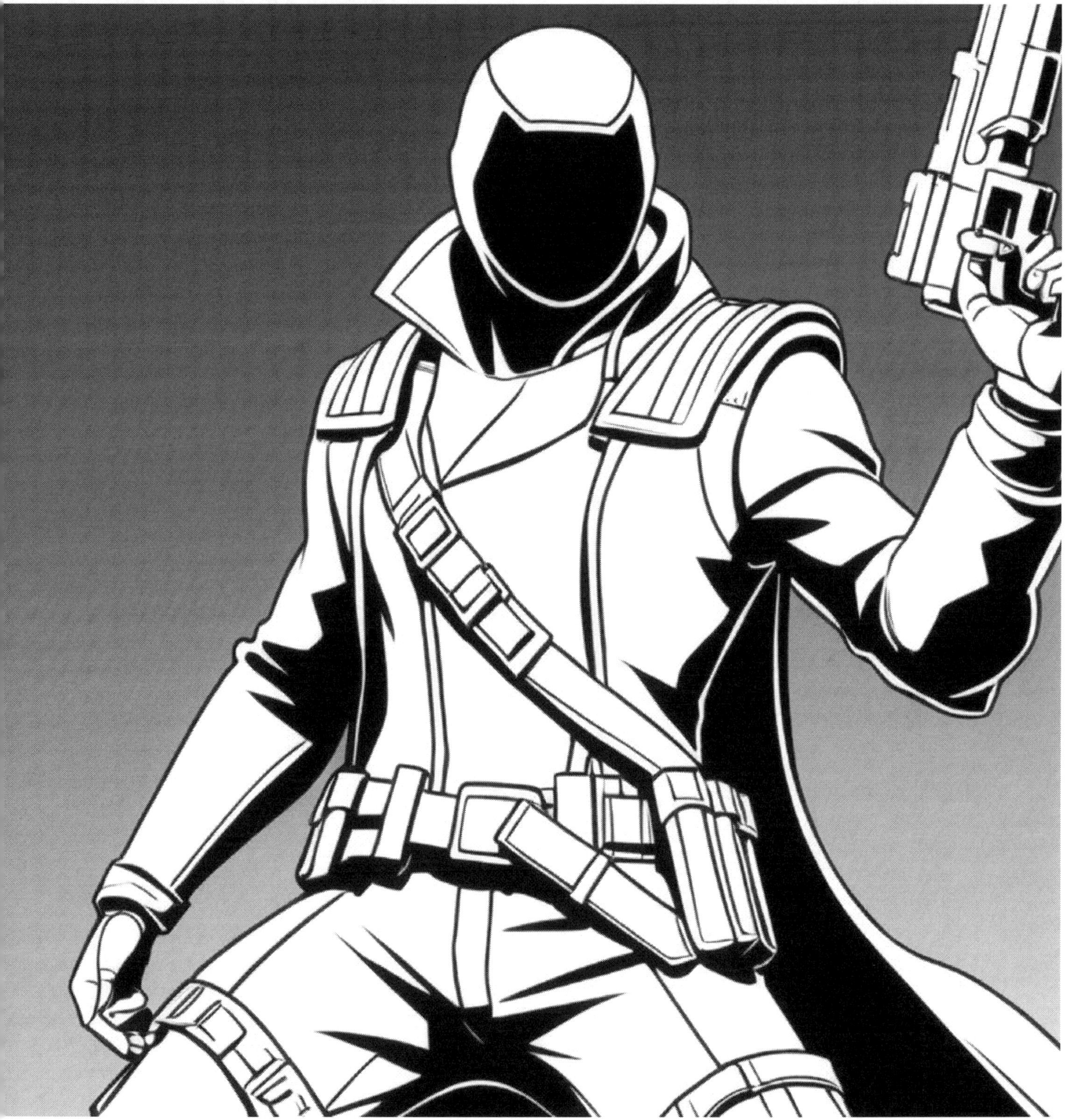

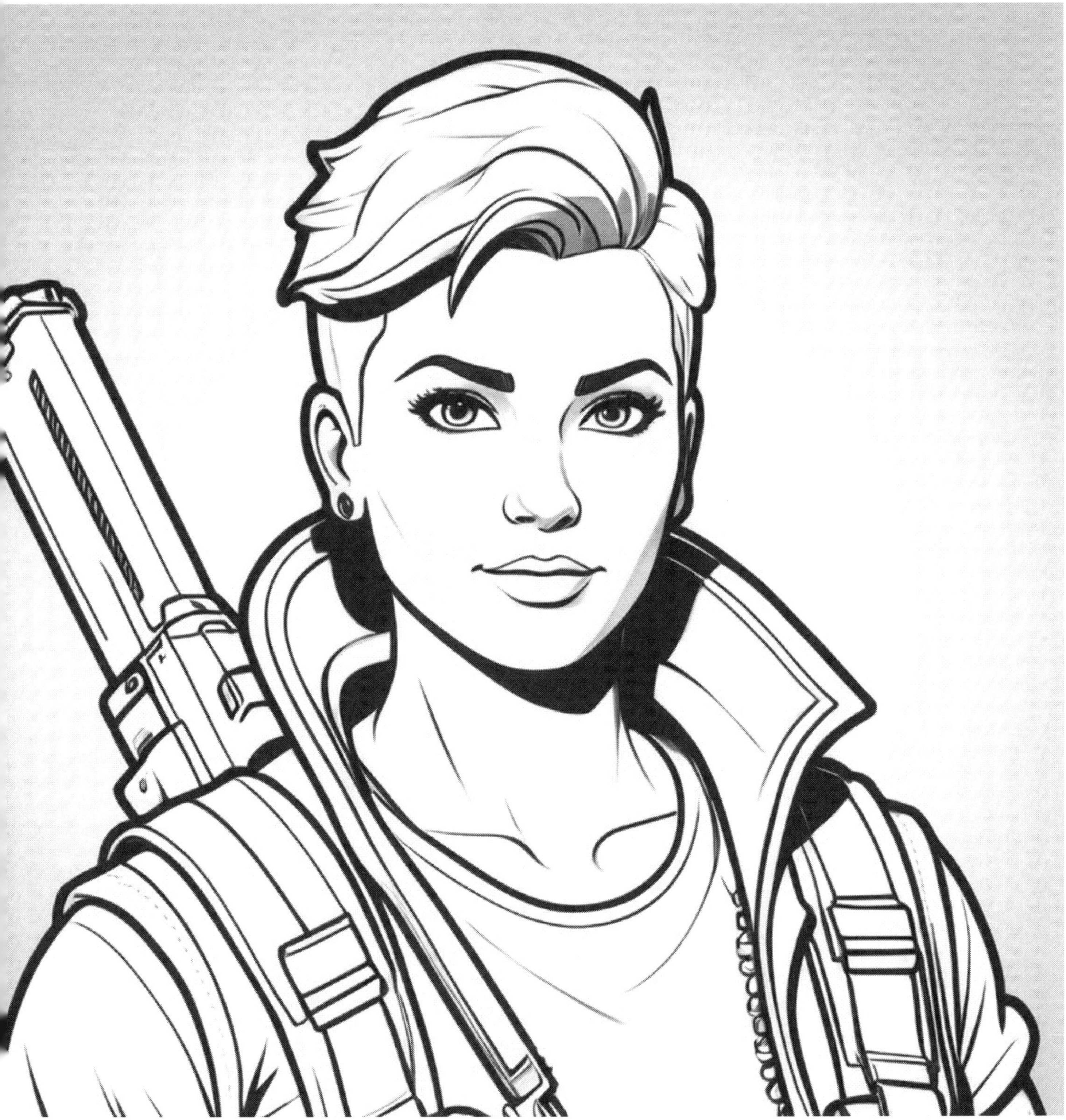

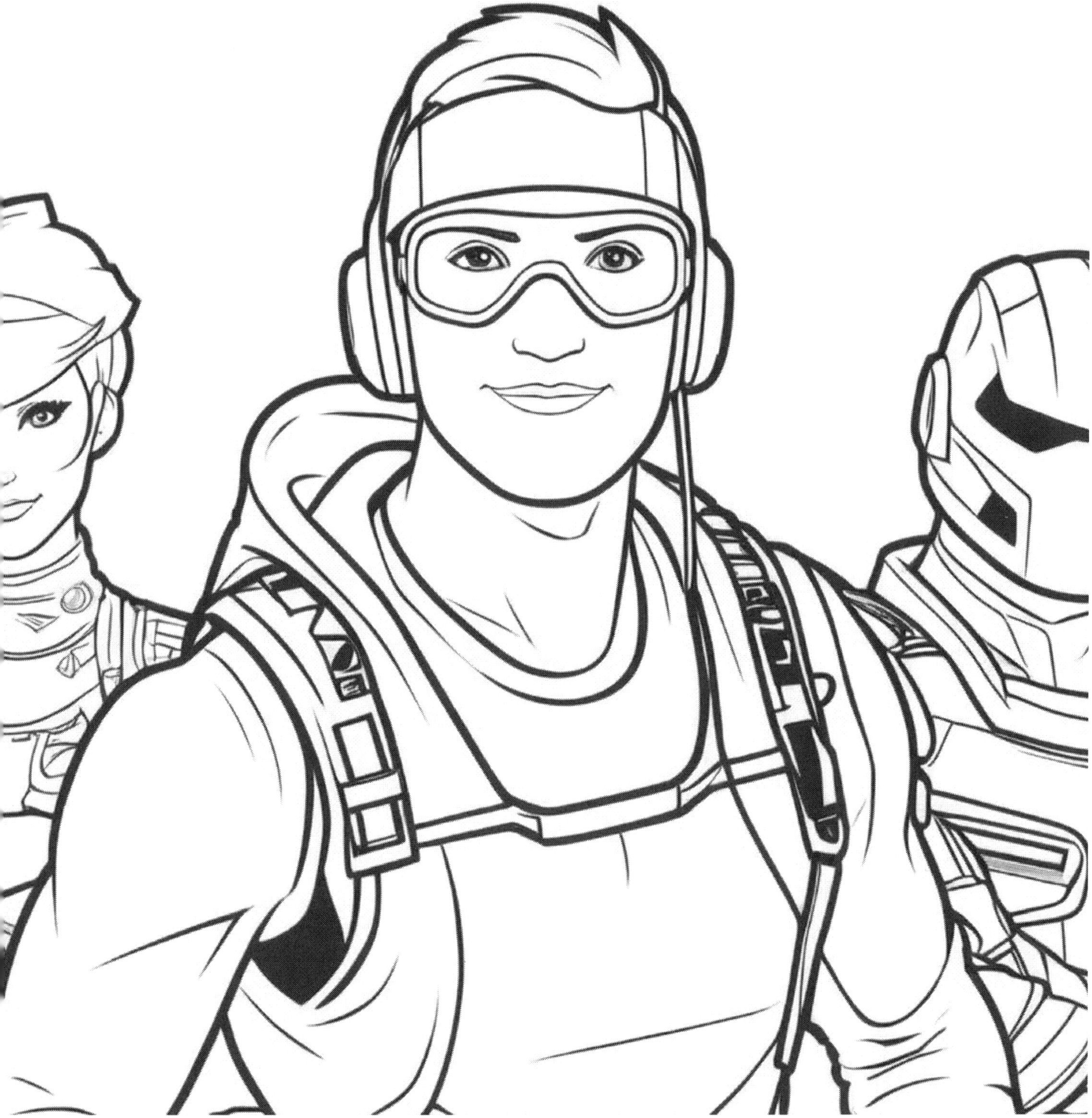

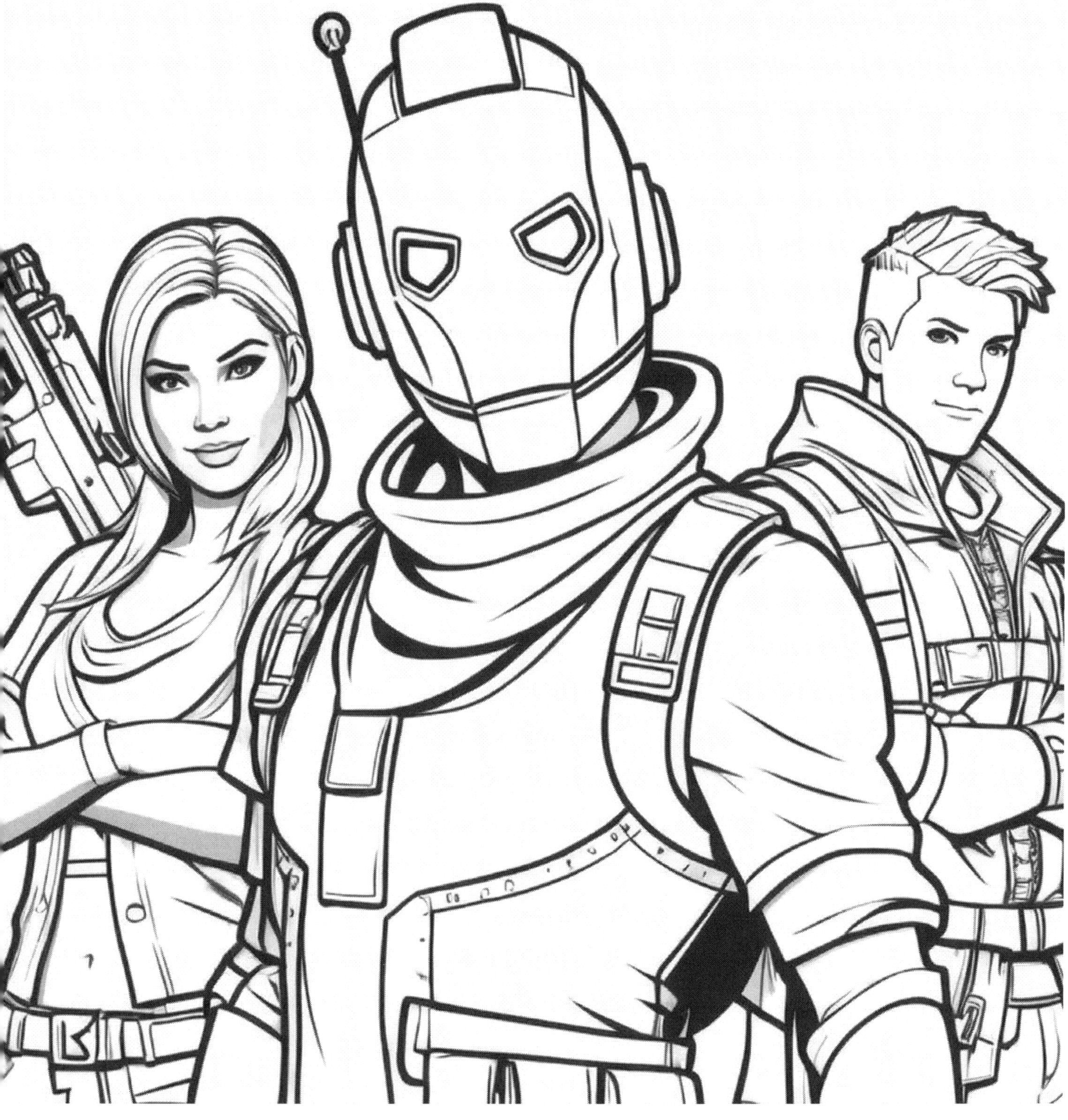

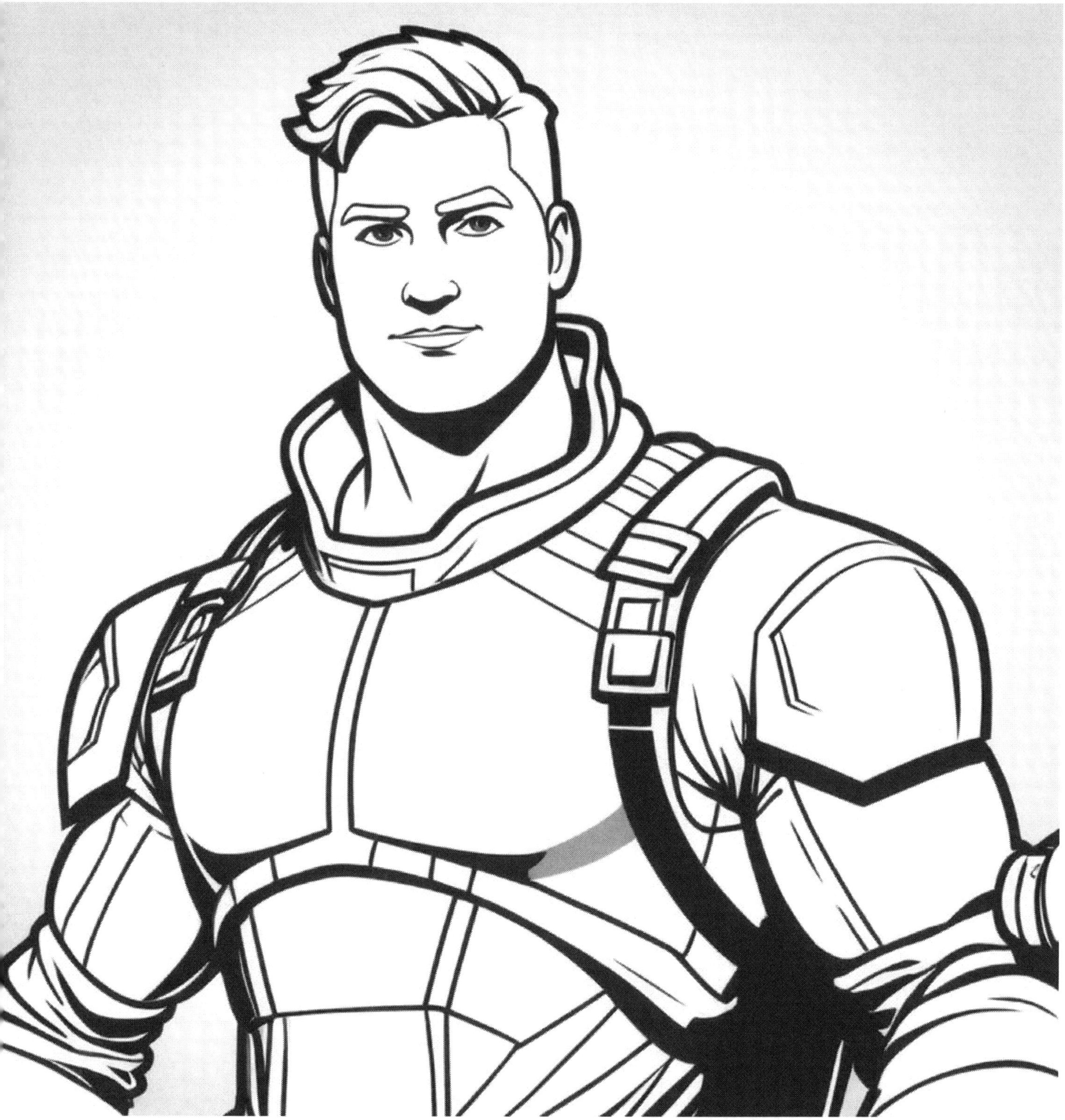

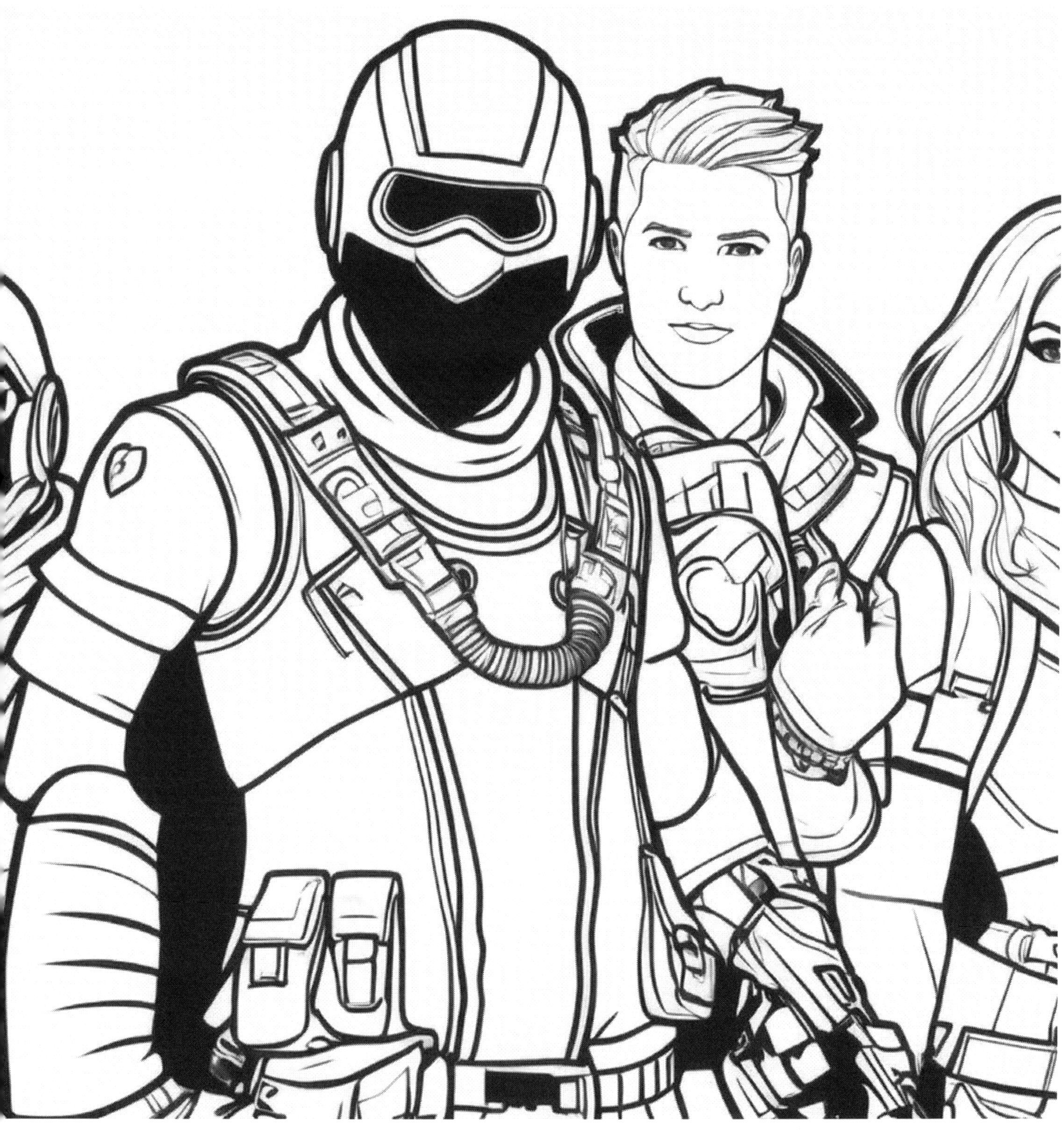

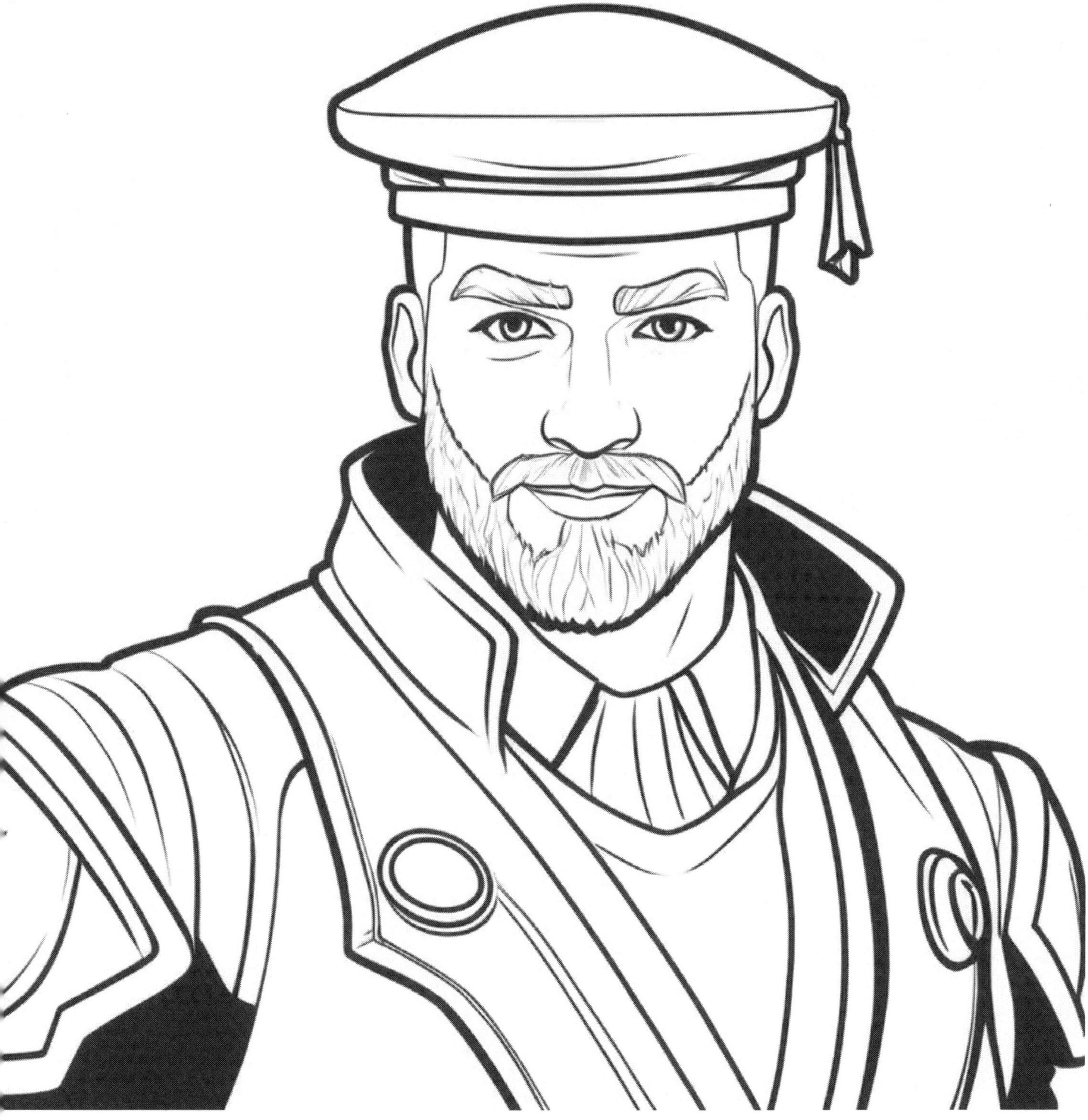

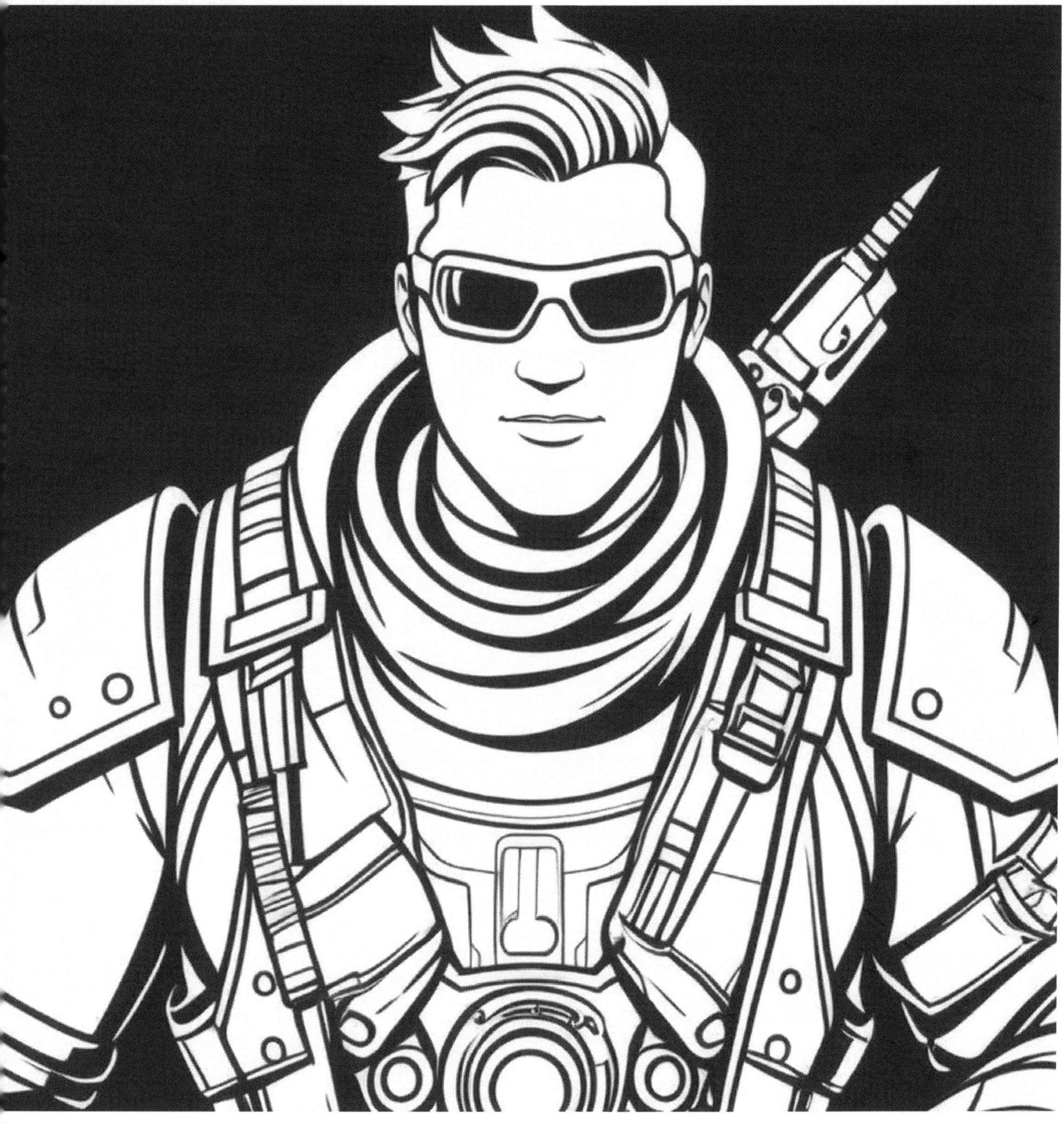

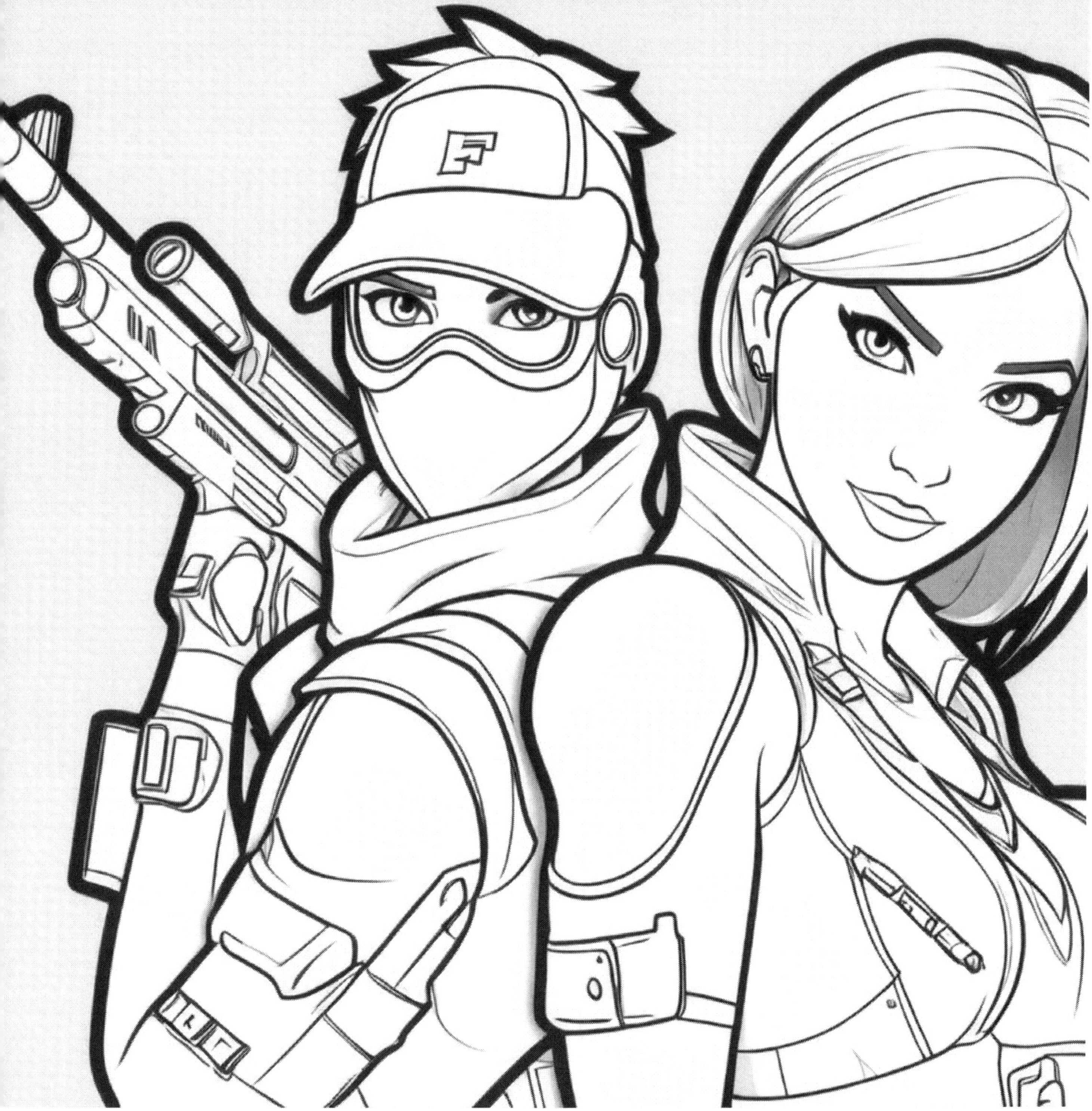
F

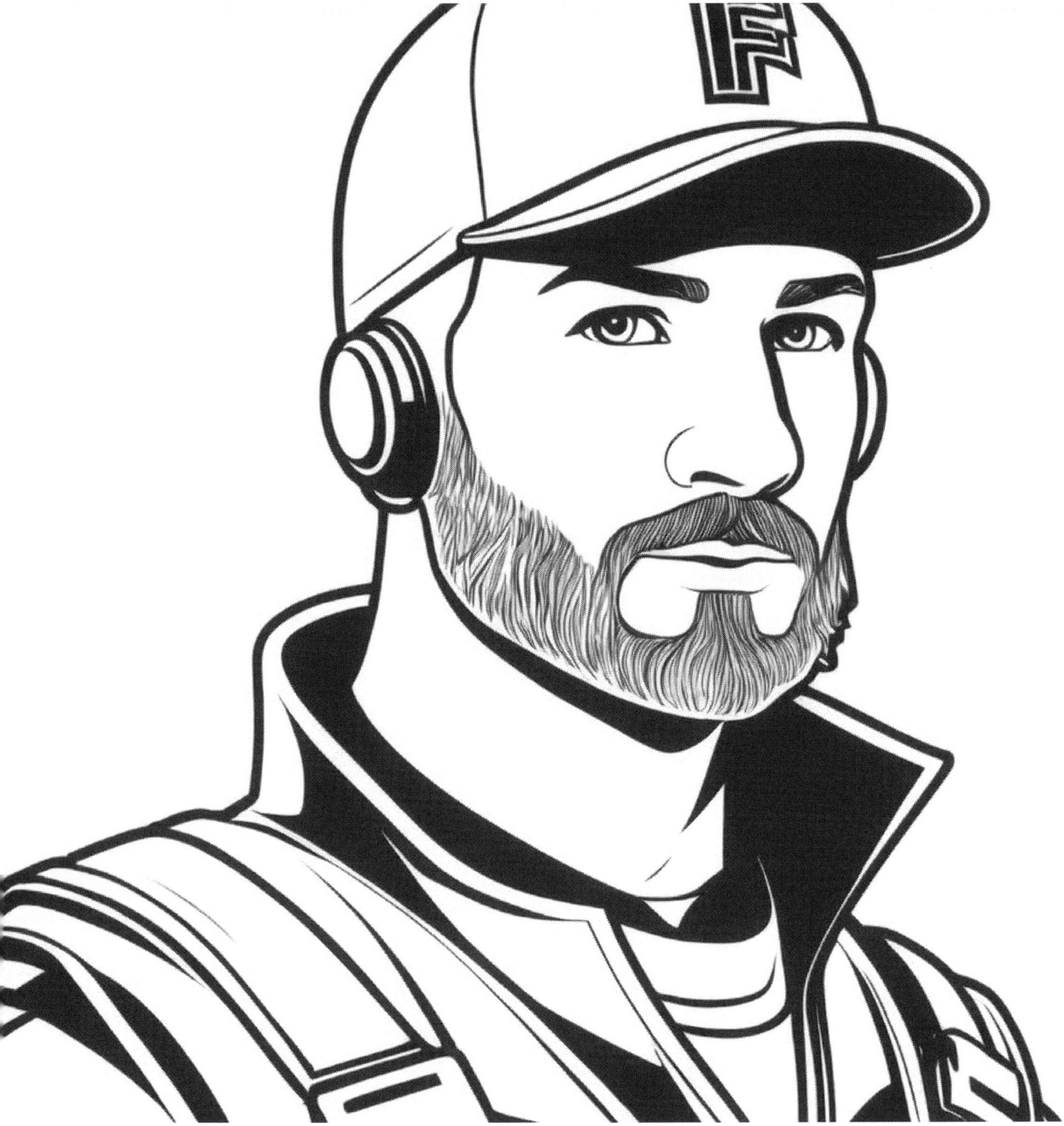

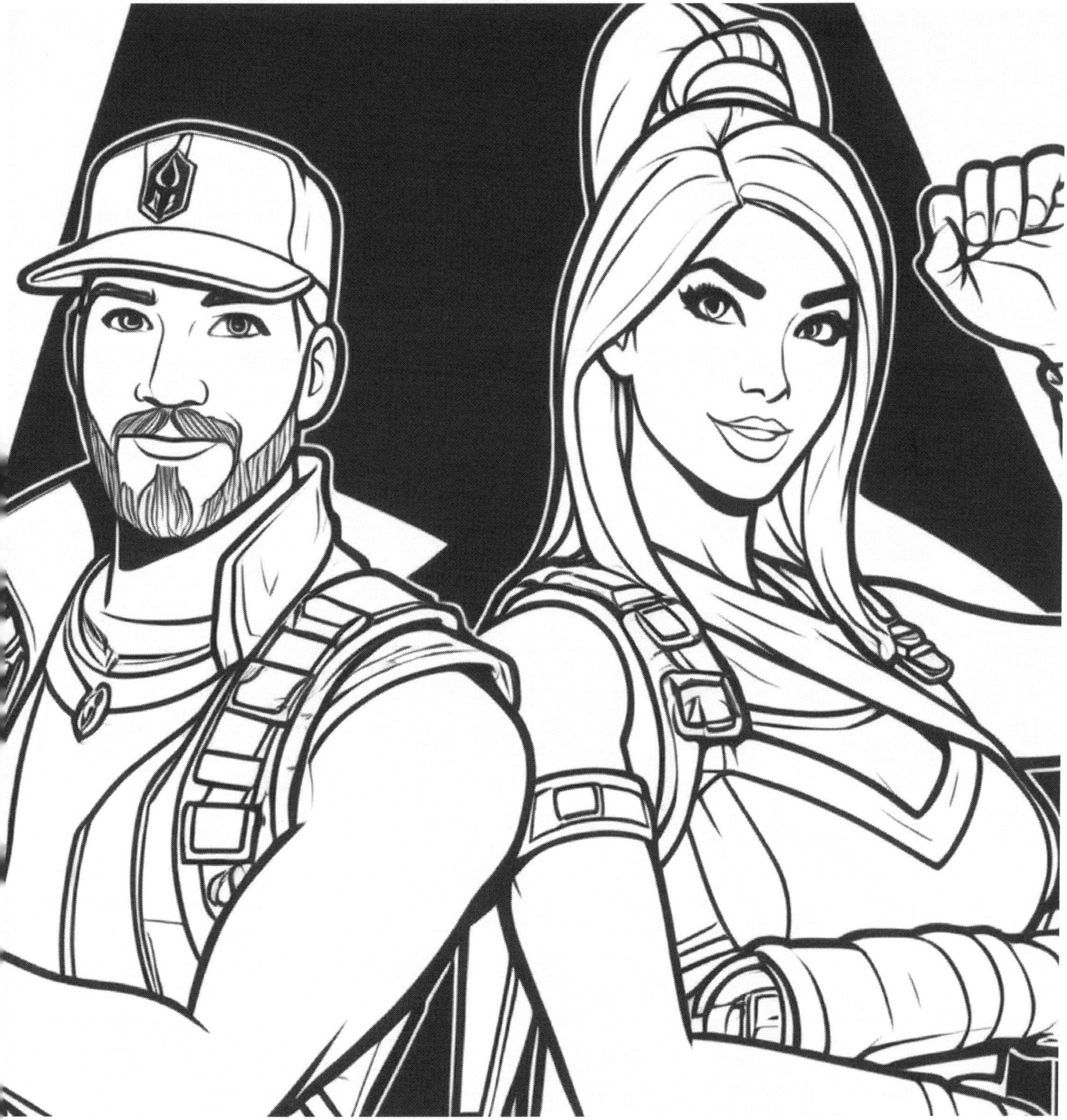

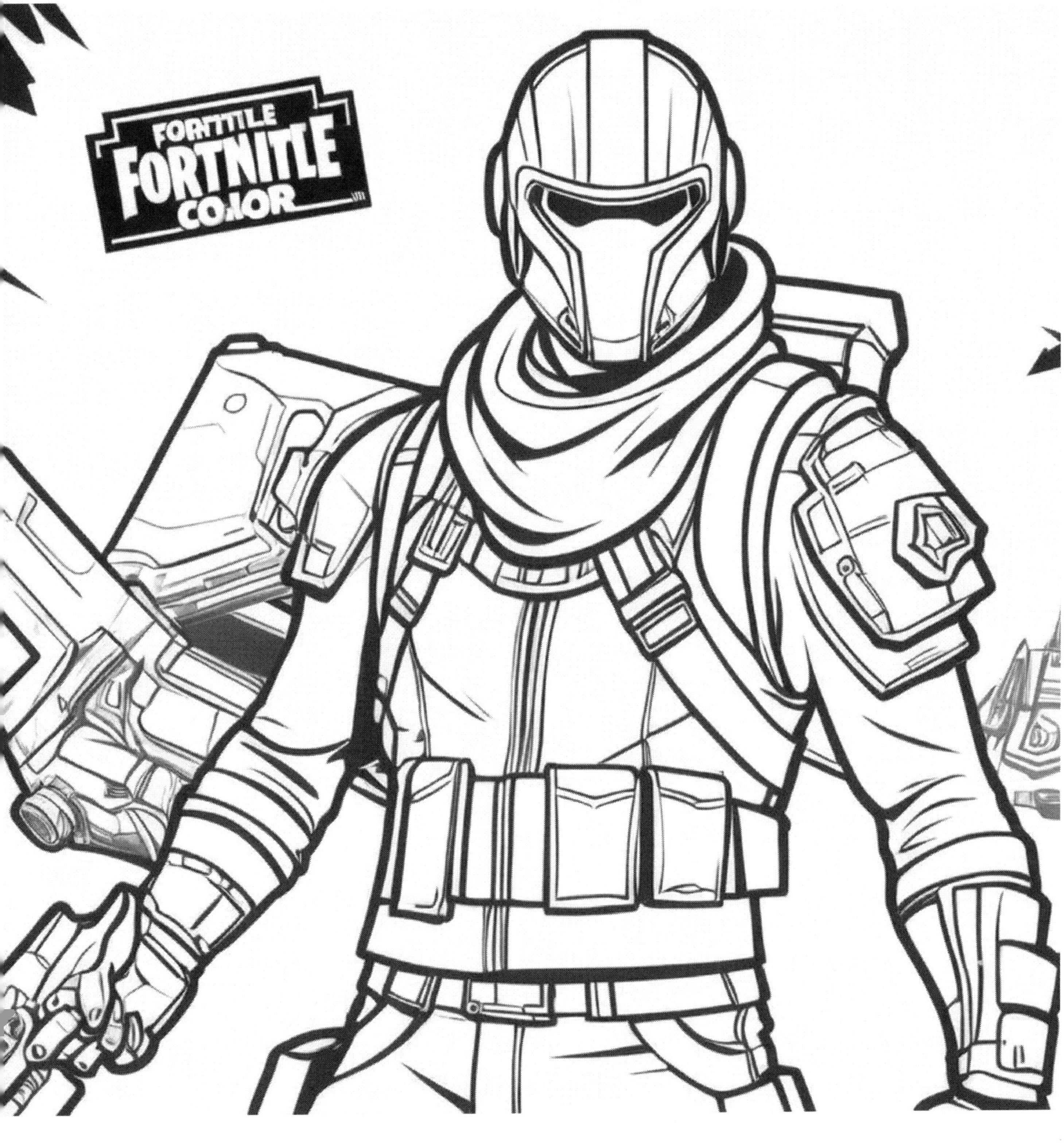
FORTNITLE

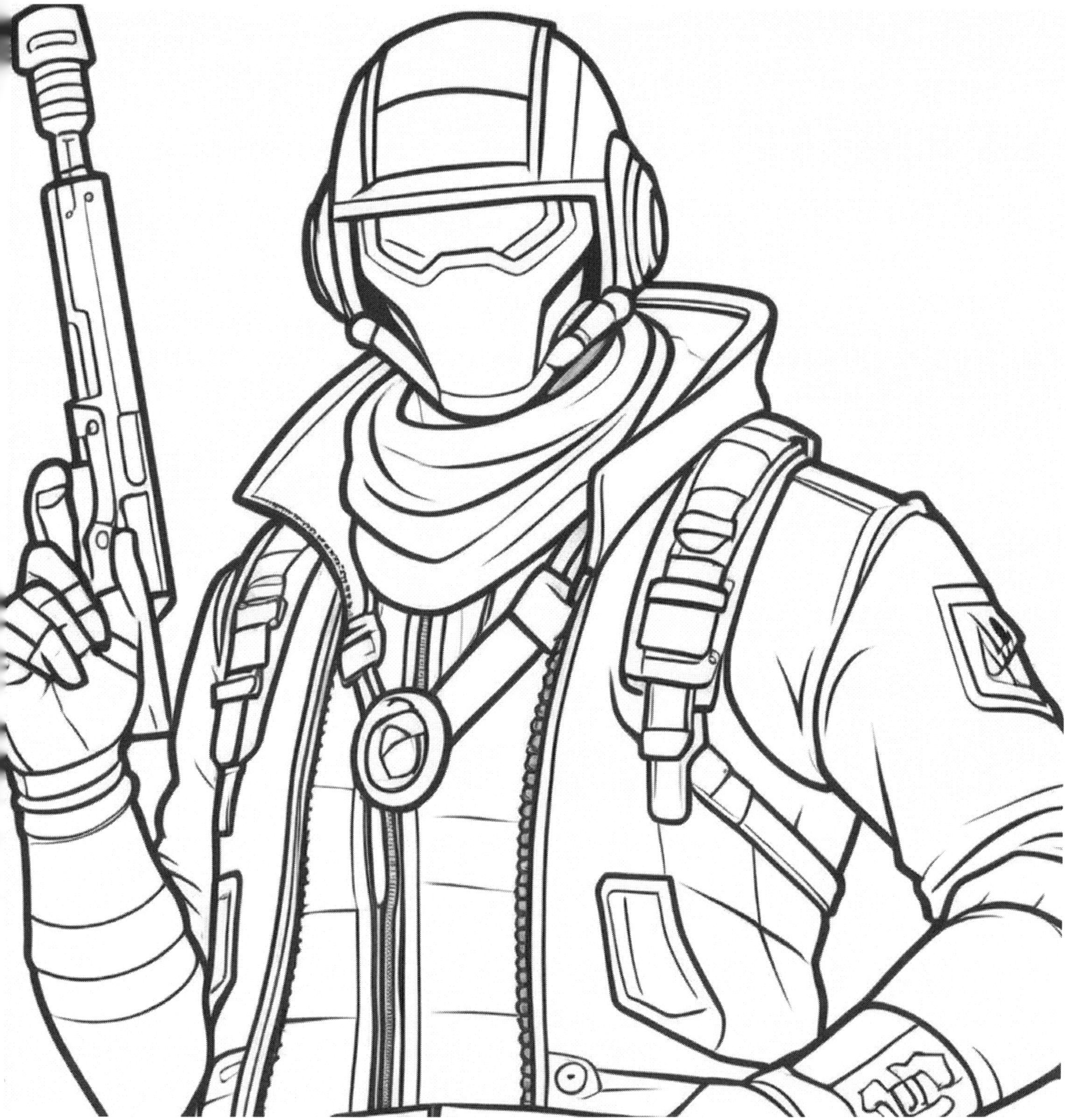

Made in United States
Troutdale, OR
11/25/2024

25281108R00058